1,000 WORDS TO SIGN

PROFESSOR GEOFFREY S. POOR

ASSOCIATE PROFESSOR
NATIONAL TECHNICAL
INSTITUTE FOR THE DEAF

1,000 WORDS TO SIGN

PROFESSOR GEOFFREY S. POOR

ASSOCIATE PROFESSOR
NATIONAL TECHNICAL
INSTITUTE FOR THE DEAF

COLLINS & BROWN

First published in 2010 by Salamander Books,
A division of the Pavilion Books Company Ltd.
43 Great Ormond Street, London WC1N 3HZ

Distributed in the United States and Canada by
Sterling Publishing Co., Inc.
1166 Avenue of the Americas
New York, NY 10036, USA

This edition published in 2018 by Collins & Brown
an imprint of the Pavilion Books Company Ltd.

All notations of errors or omissions should be addressed to Salamander Books, 43 Great Ormond Street, London WC1N 3HZ

ISBN: 978-1-911163-52-7

Reprinted 2019

Reproduction by Rival Colour
Printed in China

Author Acknowledgments
A major benefit of any language resource such as this is access—breaking down language barriers between people so that they can have access to each other's thoughts, knowledge, and ideas. I thank the National Technical Institute for the Deaf for its constant and dedicated efforts to improve access for deaf people everywhere, and for its steady support of my work over the past thirty-four years.

Photography: Eddie MacDonald
ASL Interpreter: Oliver Pouliot

Oliver Pouliot is an American Sign Language and International Sign interpreter based in London, UK. His experience ranges from a research position at the University of Rochester to contracts with the EU, EC, and UN. For the past six years he has been working in various capacities as an interpreter as well as a fine arts producer/manager. He is now the director of Overseas Interpreting, a sign language company specializing in working with deaf travelers, academics, and businesspeople. He is currently working toward his post-graduate degree in sign language interpreting as well as full qualification as a British Sign Language interpreter.

Linguistics of American Sign Language

When we use the term "sign language," we are talking about the natural visual languages that have evolved—and, as with spoken languages, are still evolving—among populations of deaf people. The research is incomplete, but there are certainly hundreds of sign languages around the world. Some are primarily used within a particular country, roughly following the geographical boundaries of that country's spoken language, while others have spread across borders or have been shipped overseas for reasons both cultural and historical. And, as with spoken languages, sign languages have dialects and regional variations, both within geographical areas and as a result of having been transplanted elsewhere.

Sign languages that are widely used, and are products of the deaf communities in the countries that use them, are a fairly recent phenomenon. This is because languages always need a certain critical mass of people who have both a need to communicate with each other and the means—contact—to do so. Because deaf people are usually a small percentage of any community, it was not until schools for the deaf began to gather significant numbers of deaf people together that sign languages became more than "home signs" from within a family, or signs that were shared within a small group of deaf people living close together in cities. In the Western world, this first happened in the mid-eighteenth century when Abbé Charles Michel De l'Épée started a school in Paris that was open to all deaf children.

The French Sign Language that evolved in the Paris school, and which then spread throughout France, was brought to America and introduced at the inception of the American School for the Deaf in Hartford, Connecticut, in 1817. It mixed with the home signs that students brought to the school, and, along with some other influences, has evolved into the beautiful and creative language we know today as American Sign Language, or ASL. It is this language that will be described in this introduction.

ASL Grammar—General Organizing Principles

Much of ASL grammar and word use is very different from English, due largely, of course, to the fact that while English uses sounds, ASL uses body movements and eyes. ASL tends to operate with what is often referred to as a "general to specific" system. ASL modifiers often come after the noun ("His new car broke down" is reordered to "His car, new, broke down"), and the structure of many sentences, especially longer ones, dictates that what the sentence is about comes before the point of the sentence ("It was impossible to find all the pins I dropped on the floor" becomes "The pins I dropped on the floor, find all, impossible"). This is just basic information about ASL word order, or syntax, and there will be more below. Before we get into that, however, let's look at some other aspects of how ASL works, so we can see how it all fits together.

Parameters of Signs

Four aspects, or parameters, are commonly used to describe ASL signs. They are: *handshape*—how the hands are configured; *location*—where the hands are in relation to the signer's body; *movement*—how the hands move; and *palm orientation*—the direction in which the hands face. Signing is more than just handshapes and movement, however, as we'll see below, and the signer's *nonmanual behaviors* (facial expression, other body movements and positioning, etc.) almost always add to the meaning and are often considered a fifth parameter.

Inflection

Linguistically, inflection means changing a word in order to change its meaning. English uses inflection a little bit ("buy" is inflected to "bought" to show past tense, for example), but English more often adds and substitutes words to change meaning. "That house is really big; actually, it's colossal." "I worked for such a long time on that project." "Cleaning the basement took all afternoon."

ASL uses a rich system of inflections instead. For example, the sign for big, two modified "L" handshapes moving away from each other in a prescribed manner, is inflected to convey *bigger*, *really big*, and *colossal* in one or more of the following ways: the hands move farther apart, the signer's facial expression changes, curves are added to the movement of the hands' separation. The sign for work has the underside of the wrist of the dominant hand's "S" handshape (let's say it's the right) coming down twice on the back of the left "S" handshape wrist. (All right/left hand references mentioned here would be reversed for a left-handed person). For "work for such a long time," the right hand hits once, slides out to the right and back again in an elliptical movement, and repeats once or twice. The longer the time, the more exaggerated the movement and the accompanying nonmanual behaviors. And to change afternoon to all afternoon is simple. The right arm with a "B" handshape, angled down about 45 degrees with palm facing out and elbow resting on the back of the left hand's "B" handshape, modifies its movement from a couple of short downward movements to a long, slow arc moving from vertical to horizontal.

Numbers have their own inflectional system. The signs for minute, day, week, and month all incorporate the index finger (the same handshape as the sign for "one") and double as the signs for one minute, one day, etc. Each of these handshapes can then be changed to the numbers from two to nine to show four days, six weeks, eight months, etc.—all with one sign. It's not until 10 and above that two signs (e.g., 10 weeks, 22 days) are needed to express these units of time.

Time Indicators and Verb Tenses

These time signs and their inflections come in handy in other ways, too. When it's necessary to specify the time when a sentence or story takes place, that "time indicator" usually comes at the beginning. For this, another aspect of the time signs' inflections comes into play. We always think of the future as being "forward" and the past being "behind us." ASL uses this concept brilliantly and eloquently. For example, to change the sign for "two weeks" (the "two" handshape sliding forward along the left palm to the fingertips) to "two weeks from now," the "two" handshape just keeps going forward past the fingertips—into the future. Two weeks ago? The "two" handshape signs two-weeks again, but this time continues back to the right and heads up toward the signer's right shoulder.

As we'll explore later in our discussion of sentence structures, this principle of establishing the time at the beginning of a sentence or paragraph has another great advantage—verbs do not carry tenses, which simplifies things greatly. The sign for "play," when in a sentence that either begins with a sign like "last year" or at any point in a narrative where the time has been established as in the past, will be translated as "played." Verbs in such a narrative will all be in the past tense until the signer changes the tense with another time indicator, at which point the verb tenses will change accordingly.

What about more complex temporal relationships, such as the past perfect tense, as in "When I applied for my job, I was surprised that they hired me, because I had just graduated from college"? This is a bit of a past tense within a past tense—the sentence is set up in the past and then refers to something that happened before that—and ASL shows this with the time line. The English sentence is ambiguous about the time of the application and hiring, inferring only that it happened in the past (applied, hired). ASL handles this with a brief movement of the right palm back over the right shoulder to establish the past, so we know that all verbs are in the simple past tense until further notice. ASL sets up the past perfect function by then signing recently before "graduate from college." This use of recently, after establishing the past, is equivalent to the English "had just [done something]."

Use of Space and Indexing

The "time line" referred to above is an example of ASL's use of temporal space. ASL also uses space to show things in their physical relationship to each other. You sometimes do this unconsciously when you speak. If you're at home and want to mention your new neighbor to a visitor, but can't recall the neighbor's name, you're likely to tilt your head toward her house or point your finger in that direction. ASL grammar takes great advantage of this awareness of space. While your spoken communication with this kind of locational information is limited to an occasional reference to a person or thing that's right around you, signers create whole casts of characters and places both present and absent, and uses the physical space around them to show what happens and the interplay between them.

Here's a simple example. You're telling someone about your friend Alan, who lives on the other side of town. You mention his name and the fact that he's your friend, and where he lives. At that point you use indexing, which is simply pointing in Alan's direction with your index finger. Pointing to that particular spot is now a pronoun—he (Alan)—and has great advantages. If you go on to mention someone else, say Walt, you'll put him in another place with indexing (the real world accuracy—whether or not you've got the N-S-E-W directions down correctly—is usually unimportant, but you must be consistent with your locations). Now, if you want to talk about Alan again, you simply point to the spot where you initially placed him. You don't need to mention his name again, because your conversation partner remembers who is where. But be careful—if you get your locations mixed up, Alan and Walt will get mixed up as well. Note that these indexed pronouns are both gender and case neutral—English has "he," "she," "him," and "her," but ASL needs only the indexed pronoun for all of these meanings. But that's just the beginning.

Space and Verb Directionality

Verbs, of course, are words of action. Someone gives something to another person, walks from one place to another place, steals something from someone, or sits on this chair or that one. English uses prepositions—from, to, on, in, etc.—to show the subjects and the direct and indirect objects. ASL uses space instead. The signs for the verbs involved—give, walk, steal, sit—inflect to show their subjects and objects. How? They change their direction of movement.

Suppose you want to tell someone this story: Your brother Mike lives in Chicago and your sister Lily lives in Florida. Last year you gave Mike a very funny picture of Lily taken when she was a child. Mike thought about mailing it to her, but he realized he'd be flying to Florida on business in a few weeks and could give it to her himself. When he did, and Lily found out that Mike had gotten the picture from you, she called you to talk and laugh about the picture.

We know that you'll put Mike in one place with indexing (to the left is sort of a default, and unless you're dealing with someone present, it doesn't matter and you'll put Lily in another place—to the right normally follows. Now that you and your conversation partner know who and where everyone is, space and directionality allow you to explain what happens by using just a handful of signs and their graceful movements. First you establish when the story takes place—you modify the sign for "year" to mean "last year," and then use your indexed "he" to refer to Mike. Right now we'll just describe how the verbs work. You start the action by inflecting the sign "give" so that it moves from you to Mike in Chicago; Mike, thinking about it, inflects the sign for "send" so that it moves from him (to your left) to Lily (to your right). Then, thinking again but this time about giving it to her in person, inflects the sign for "fly" so that it moves from him to Lily. Well, you can see how this progresses: verb signs move from person to person, carrying all kinds of information along for the ride. Lily asks Mike where he got the picture, and Mike tells her you gave it to him. Lily calls you and you have a good laugh (it's a good thing she thinks the picture is funny, too).

There's another advantage to this use of space, and it appears over and over in ASL: economy of motion. Verb directionality and indexing together *include* the subjects and objects of the verbs through the start and end points of their movement, which means that it's often unnecessary to sign the people and place names again, and only rarely the prepositions. Once locations and the time have been established, an English sentence like "I gave her the letter" can be translated with two signs (LETTER I-GIVE-TO-HER). Just one sign can be used for "She called me" (SHE-CALL-ME), and for "I'll fly from Chicago to Florida" (merely the sign for an airplane moving from our established Chicago to Florida). And again, we know this happened two years ago, so there's no need to burden the verb with a tense. And why is this economy of motion important? While ears are passive receptors of sound, with no work required on the listener's part (remember, we're talking about hearing the sounds of language with the ear, not deciphering them with the brain), the eye functions largely as a muscle for the purposes of following a sign's movement and focusing on it. In other words, eyes can get tired. Making skillful use of the signing space and reducing the number of signs helps to construct a clear, easy-to-understand message.

Sentence Structures

For short sentences, the basic English syntactical arrangement of subject-verb-object (SVO) can often be used in ASL. "The cat ate the fish" can be signed as CAT EAT FISH. (The past tense will have already been established, of course.) However, for longer sentences, and for some particular types of sentences, some significant rearrangement is necessary.

Topic/Comment

When we use the word "subject" in analyzing an English sentence, we often mean the subject of the sentence's verb. In "The cat ate the fish," the subject of the verb eat is *cat*. However, the subject of the sentence—what the sentence is basically about—may not be the same as a particular verb's subject. Although "I saw a turtle swim across a pond" starts with "I," the sentence is not about me—the turtle enjoys that honor. So instead of describing ASL sentences in terms of subject and object, we use "topic/comment." The topic is what the sentence is about, and may include some additional information about the topic, and the comment is the point of the sentence—what the signer has to say about the topic or what prompts her to say anything at all about it. In our sentence about the turtle, the reason I decided to tell someone about this event is that I saw it. There's not much conversational value in "a turtle swam across a pond."

In short sentences, ASL signers have the option of using either SVO or topic/comment structure, but for longer sentences, topic/comment structure is required. All ASL sentence structures require the use of very specific facial expressions. Without the correct use of these facial expressions, they aren't sentences at all; they're simply collections of words, and are either muddled or outright incomprehensible. In general, the facial expression at the *beginning* of the sentence indicates what the topic is, and the facial expression at the end of the sentence indicates what kind of sentence it is—declarative, yes/no question, information question, etc.

We'll start with a simple declarative statement in topic/comment structure. The topic is always indicated by raised eyebrows. The English sentence: "My expensive new car broke down yesterday" would be signed this way: *YESTERDAY, MY CAR, NEW, EXPENSIVE*, BREAK-DOWN. All the words in italics—the topic—are signed with raised eyebrows, and when the signer reaches BREAK-DOWN, he drops his eyebrows and adds a slight head nod.

Yes/No Questions

Here's a good example of the importance of facial expression in ASL: yes/no questions. These are questions that request only one of three answers: yes, no, or some variation of uncertainty (maybe, I don't know, etc.). They require raised eyebrows at the end. The sentences "There are many people waiting for the bus" and "Are there many people waiting for the bus?" are both signed with the exact same signs, and it's only the raised eyebrows at the end of the second sentence that indicate it's a question. But, you say, don't the raised eyebrows mean the sentence topic? Yes, they do, but only at the *beginning* of the sentence. If the eyebrows remain raised at the end of the sentence, it becomes a question: using our convention of *ITALICS* to indicate raised eyebrows, the statement *PEOPLE WAIT FOR BUS*, MANY becomes the question *PEOPLE WAIT FOR BUS, MANY*?

Information Questions

These questions demand more of an answer, and include a word such as *why, when, where, what, how*, etc. For these sentences, the question sign is at or near the end, where it effectively forms the point of the sentence. The question sign must be accompanied by furrowed eyebrows, which we'll indicate here in **BOLD**. "Where's the new toy I gave the baby?" is signed *NEW TOY, I GIVE-TO BABY,* **WHERE**? And, of course, because a sentence like this will likely be signed during a conversation about a baby whose location will have been established, the direction of motion in the sign GIVE-TO will be toward the baby. These facial expressions for questions, by the way, are quite similar in function to changes in voice intonation when spoken questions are asked. Listen to people asking yes/no and information questions and you'll notice distinct and consistent patterns. These are merely conventions with English, however, and not grammatical rules as the corresponding facial expressions are with ASL.

Conditional Sentences

"I'm going to the game tomorrow if the ticket price goes down." "If the ticket price goes down, I'm going to the game." English gives us these two options for structuring a conditional (if…then…) sentence. In ASL, because of the topic/comment principle and facial expression, the "if" clause always comes first. One advantage of this is that using the separate sign for "if" is optional and often not used—economy of motion. The initial, conditional clause is indicated by our old friend, the raised eyebrows: *TICKET PRICE REDUCE*, GO-TO GAME I. Conditional questions ("Will you go to the game if the ticket price goes down?" "What will you do if the ticket price goes down?") follow all the principles of structure and facial expression explained above (*TICKET PRICE REDUCE, GO-TO GAME YOU? TICKET PRICE REDUCE,* **DO-WHAT YOU**?)

Rhetorical Questions

Rhetorical questions are meant to be answered not by the person being addressed but by the person who poses the question, and again, the facial expression is the key: the question sign is signed not with furrowed brows but with raised eyebrows. In English, rhetorical questions are primarily for formal situations and/or emphasis ("What do we want? Progress." "Why did the chicken cross the road? More bugs."). ASL uses rhetorical questions much more frequently and casually. The English "My attempt to go by boat across the Atlantic failed because my boat slowly started to sink" is very cumbersome and unnatural if translated as *GO-BY-BOAT ACROSS ATLANTIC*, I TRY, FAIL BECAUSE BOAT SINK-SLOWLY. What works instead is *GO-BY-BOAT ACROSS ATLANTIC*, I TRY, FAIL; *WHY?* BOAT SINK-SLOWLY.

Classifiers

Classifiers are generally considered absent from English, but are a big part of ASL (and some spoken languages). In ASL, classifiers are handshapes used to represent nouns and include information on size and shape, location, and movement, or sometimes all of these. Since classifiers can be applied to many things (the "three" handshape, for example, can be used to indicate any land or water vehicle), they must be labeled just before or after their use, (boat, car, etc.), unless what they're representing is clear from the context. In our sentence above about the ill-fated journey across the ocean, you may have noticed that only one sign is needed to convey that the boat is sinking slowly. That's because the "three" handshape, representing the boat, will actually move slowly downward as the sentence ends. A faster movement means a faster sink.

Putting All This Together

ASL sometimes seems involved and complicated when analyzed this way; all languages do. Here are some hints for putting it into practice.

• Have a physical image in your head. When you sign about people, things, and places, picture them in your mind as being in specific places. Don't worry about accuracy; just go with your gut instinct. Quick now: where is your car? That's all you need to get started.

• Before you start to sign a sentence, pause just a second and figure out what it's about. Sign that with your eyebrows raised, and you'll be pleasantly surprised how the rest of it will flow.

• Be an actor. Let what's going on inside you show on your face.

• And, perhaps most important of all, watch deaf people sign. Learning any language is as much a process of absorbing it as it is of memorizing its vocabulary and grammar.

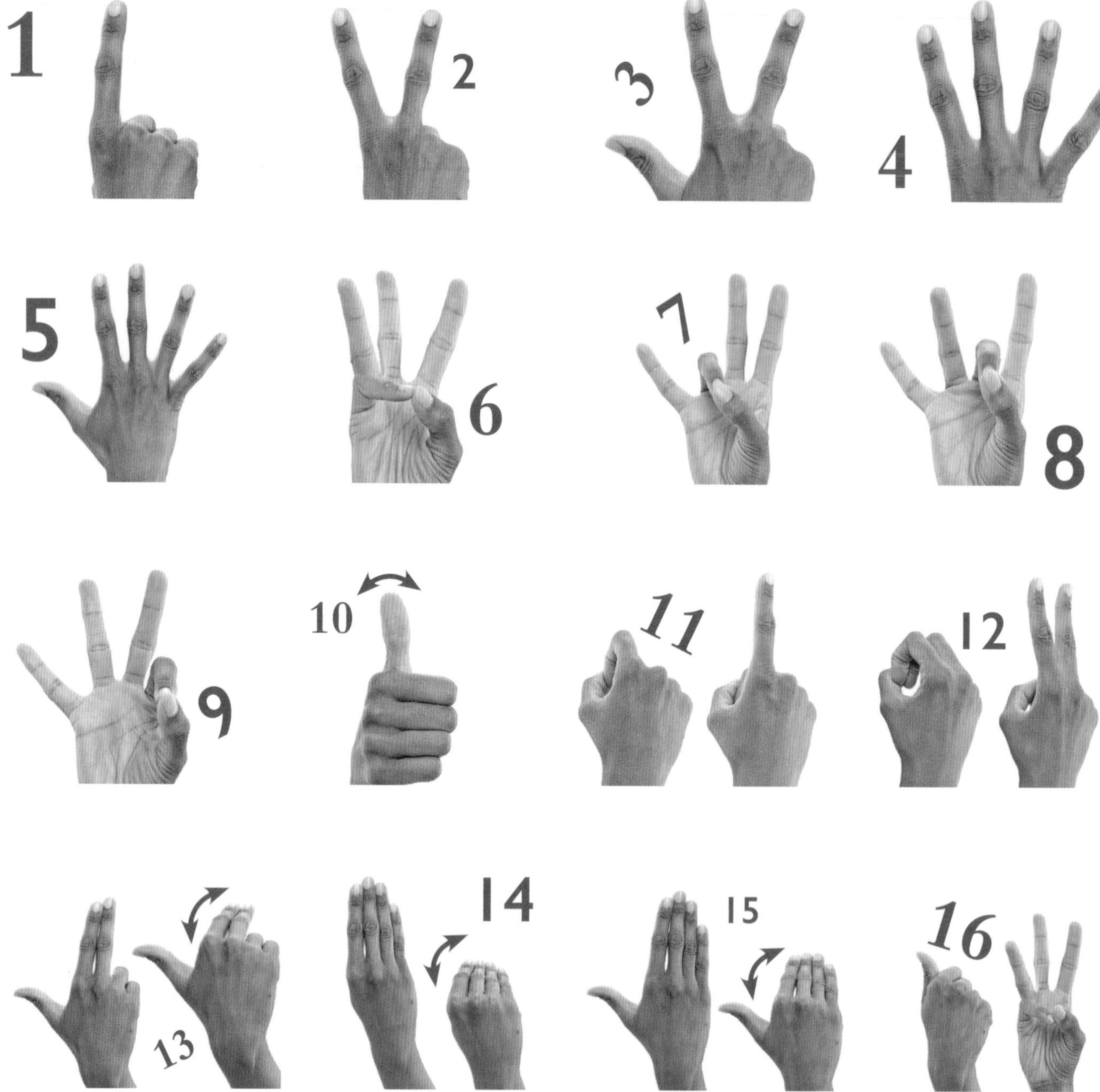
1
2
3
4
5
6
7
8
9
10
11
12
13
14
15
16

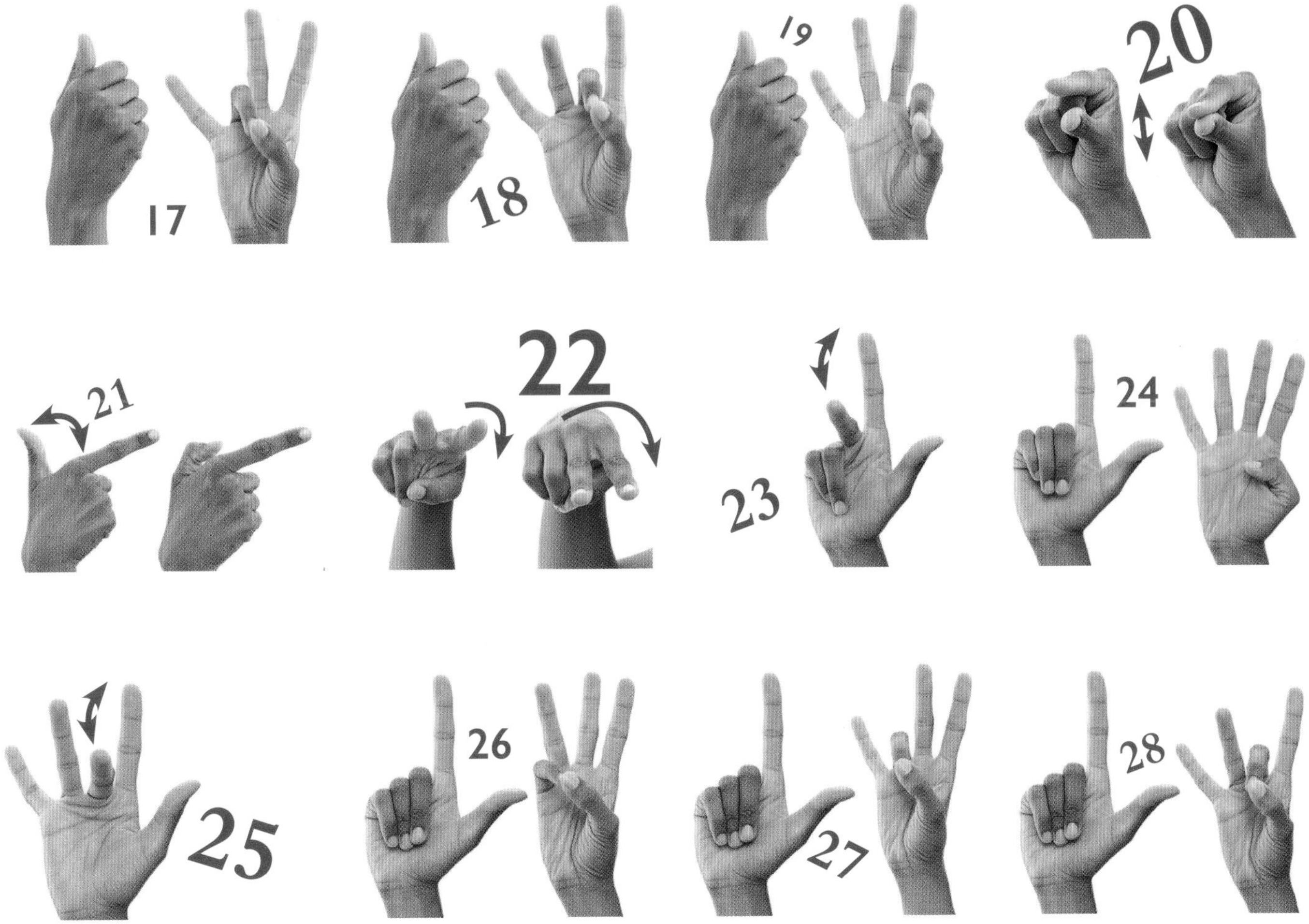

17
18
19
20
21
22
23
24
25
26
27
28

29
30

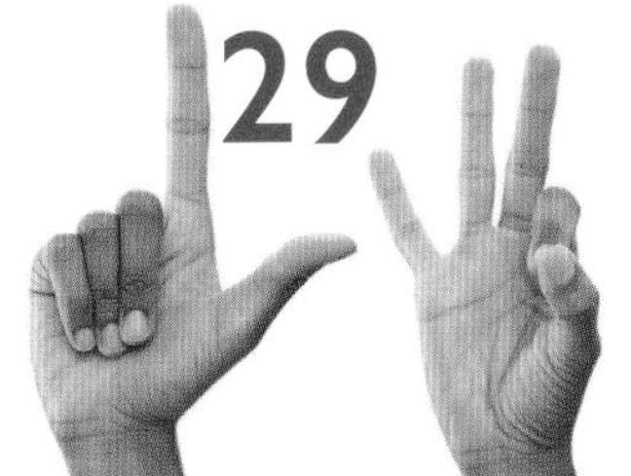

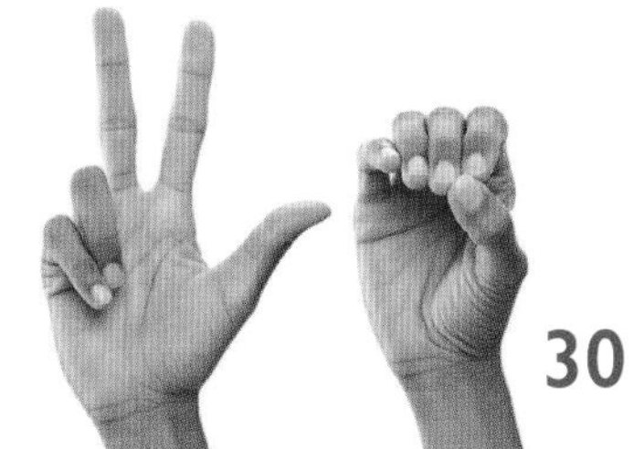

NUMBERS

These photographs show what is seen by the person watching the signer.

alphabet

days of the week

MONDAY	TUESDAY	WEDNESDAY	THURSDAY	FRIDAY	SATURDAY	SUNDAY	WEEKEND
Rotate "M" handshape from elbow using small clockwise circular motions.	Rotate "T" handshape from elbow using small clockwise circular motions.	Rotate "W" handshape from elbow using small clockwise circular motions.	Handshape moves from "T" to "H."	Rotate "F" handshape from elbow using small clockwise circular motions.	Rotate fist from elbow using small clockwise circular motions.	Palms out; hands move from chin height to chest height.	With index finger extended, slide right hand along left palm; change to flat handshape and bring down left fingertips at a right angle.

colors

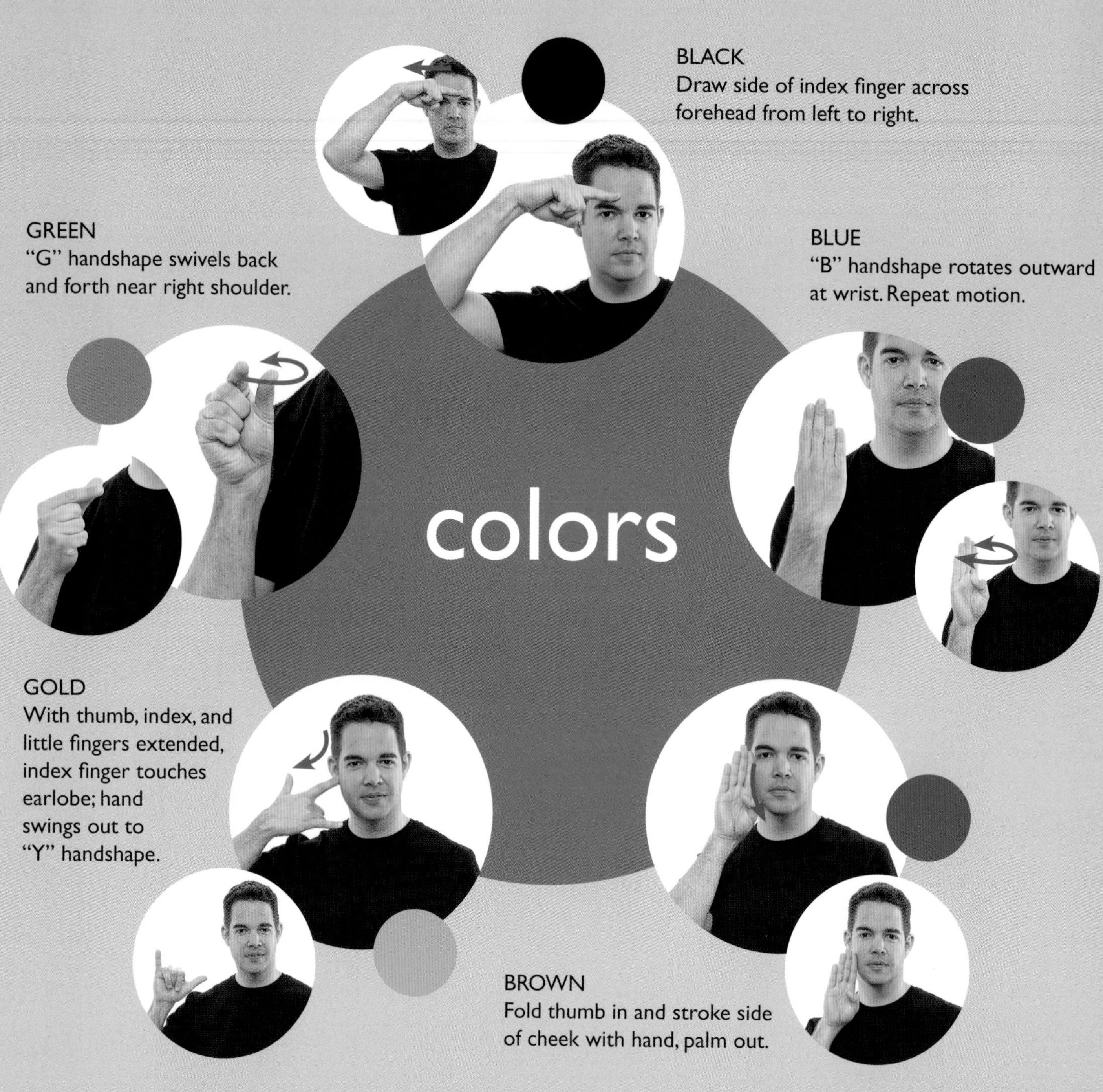

BLACK
Draw side of index finger across forehead from left to right.

BLUE
"B" handshape rotates outward at wrist. Repeat motion.

BROWN
Fold thumb in and stroke side of cheek with hand, palm out.

GOLD
With thumb, index, and little fingers extended, index finger touches earlobe; hand swings out to "Y" handshape.

GREEN
"G" handshape swivels back and forth near right shoulder.

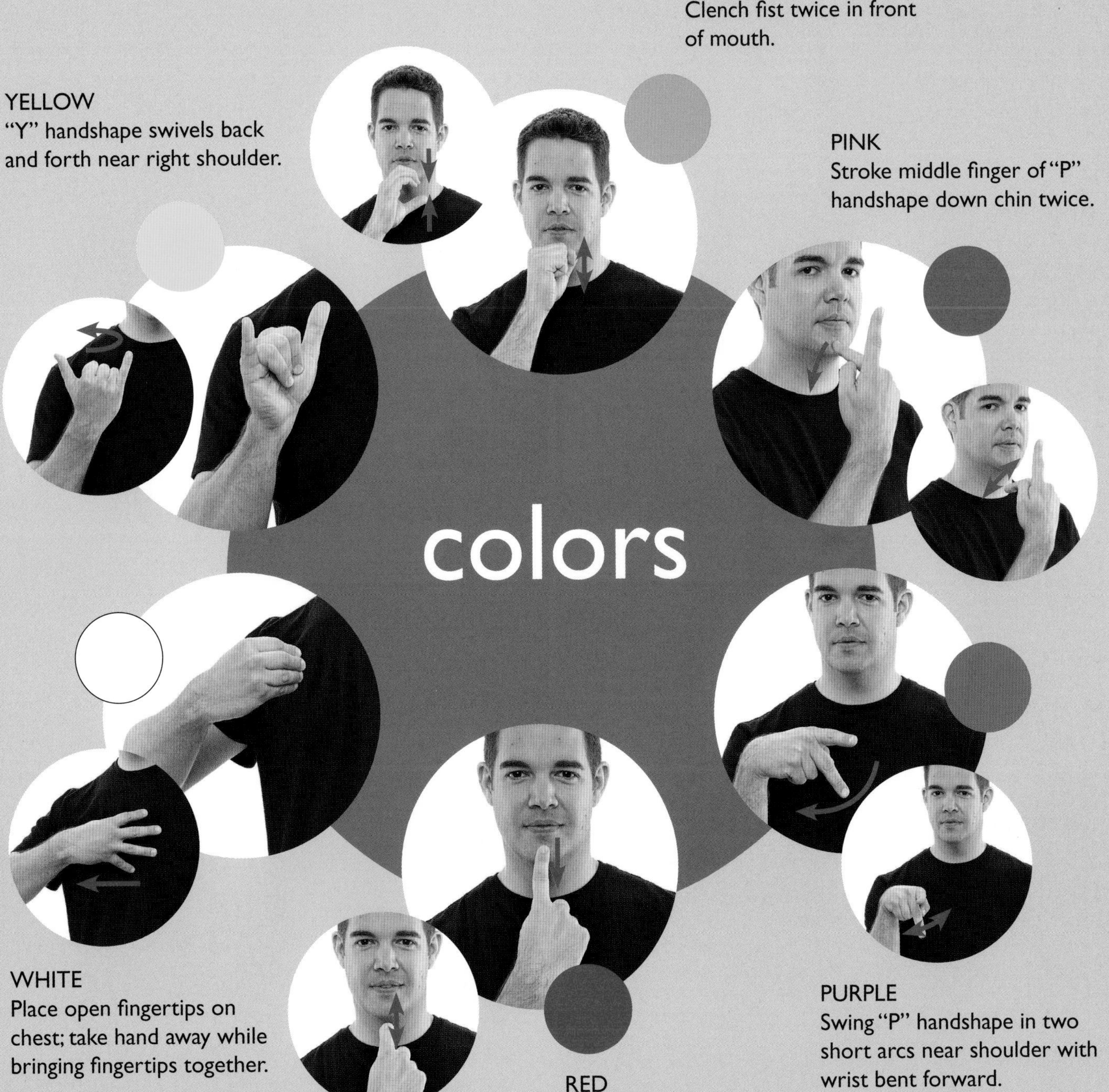

ORANGE
Clench fist twice in front of mouth.

YELLOW
"Y" handshape swivels back and forth near right shoulder.

PINK
Stroke middle finger of "P" handshape down chin twice.

WHITE
Place open fingertips on chest; take hand away while bringing fingertips together.

PURPLE
Swing "P" handshape in two short arcs near shoulder with wrist bent forward.

RED
Crook finger twice from chin.

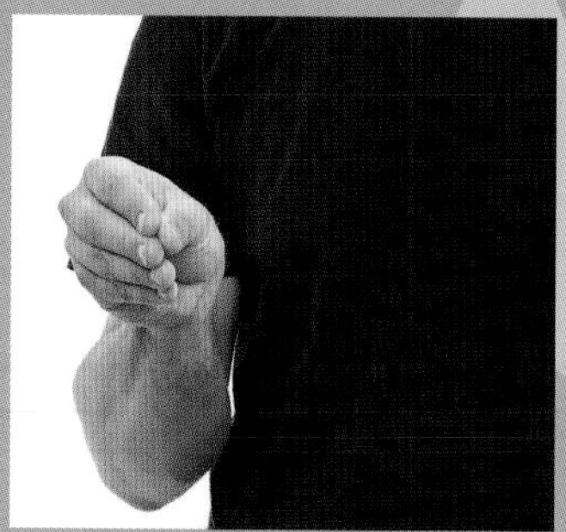

AFRICA
Partially open hand arcs to the right while closing.

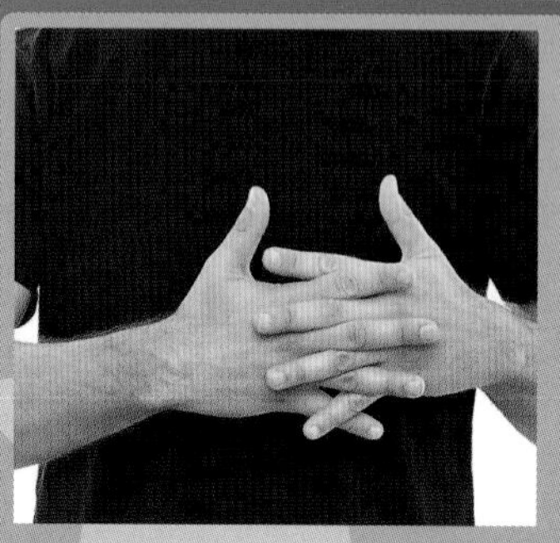
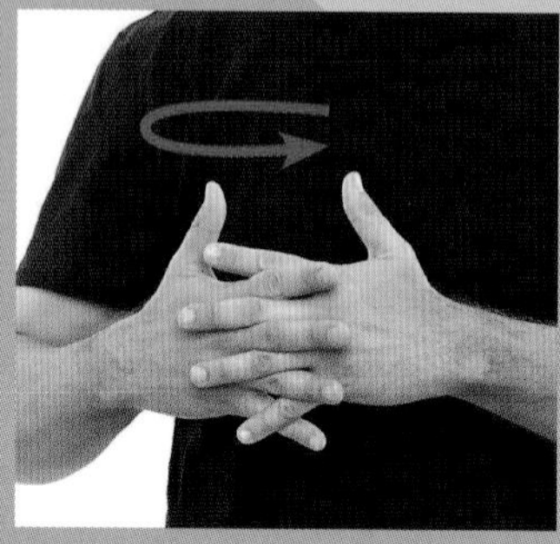

AMERICA
Interlock fingers in front of body with thumbs outstretched; rotate arms clockwise.

AUSTRALIA
Hands move up, out, and down, flicking middle fingers out from thumbs at the end.

countries

CANADA
Stretch out thumb and tap on body twice between shoulder and chest.

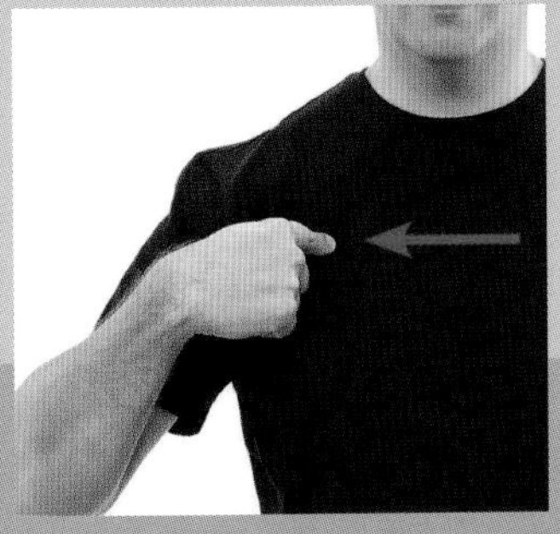

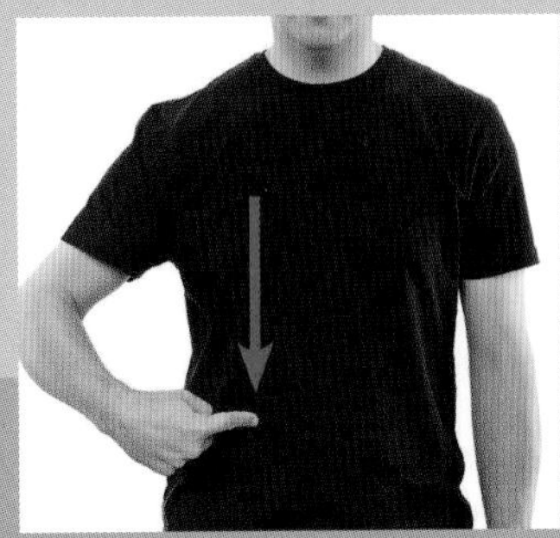

CHINA
Tip of index finger draws a right-angle across body from shoulder to shoulder and down to waist.

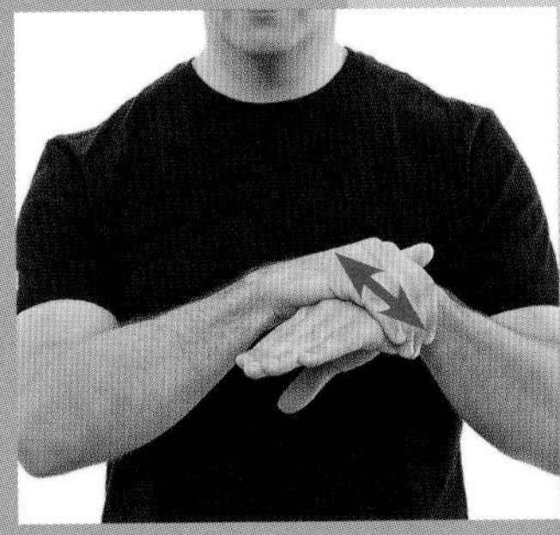

ENGLAND
Right cupped hand grasps back of left hand and shakes twice lightly.

EUROPE
Rotate "E" handshape in and bring to side of forehead.

FRANCE
"F" handshape swings inward and to the right.

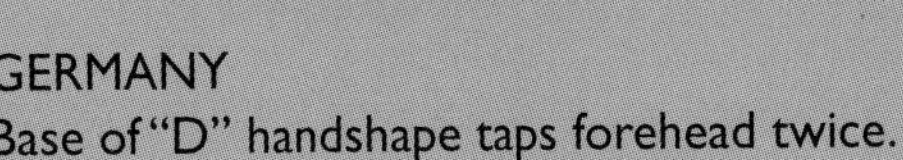

GERMANY
Base of "D" handshape taps forehead twice.

INDIA
Extended thumb twists down twice while pressing middle of forehead.

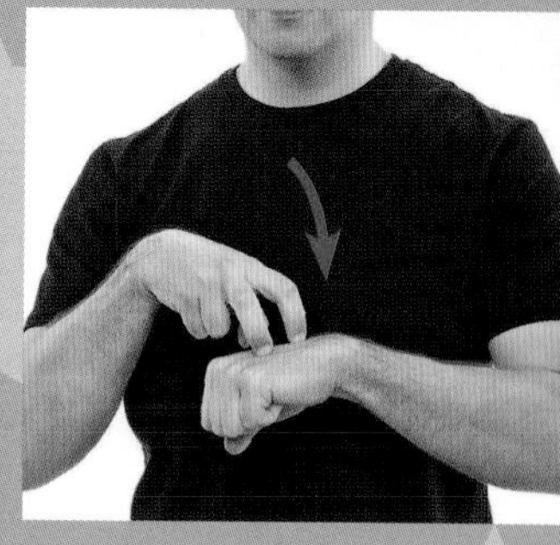

IRELAND
Hook middle and index fingers, circle, and bring down on back of hand.

ITALY
Thumb and crooked index finger move to the right and down.

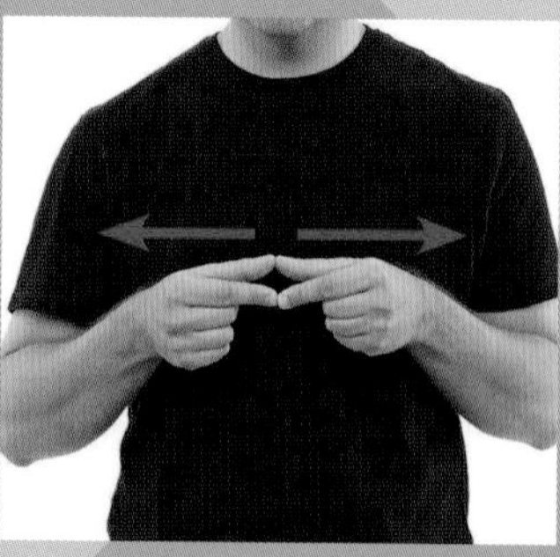

JAPAN
Join hands using tips of thumbs and index fingers; pull hands apart while closing fingers; repeat.

MEXICO
Index finger of "V" handshape touches forehead above right eye, then flicks out twice.

RUSSIA
Side of index finger slides to the right along chin and moves down.

SPAIN
Thumb and crooked index finger touch chest near shoulder, then rotate out 90 degrees and touch again.

ABANDON

Palms sweep up and face out

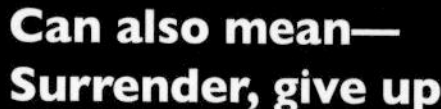

Can also mean—
Surrender, give up

ABOUT (CONCERNING)

Index finger circles out, down, and around closed left hand.

Can also mean—
Concerning

ABOVE

Right hand arcs slightly to the right and up from left.

ACCEPT

Open out hands, move inward, and close against chest.

ACCIDENT (VEHICULAR)

Open hands close and meet as fists.

ACT

Alternately brush thumbs against chest with small inward circles.

Can also mean—Play, theater, show, drama, perform

ADD TO

Move open right hand up and in, closing to meet left hand.

ADDRESS

Move both hands, with thumbs upward, against chest in two circular motions.

ADVERTISE

Right fist moves forward and opens from in front of left fist. Repeat motion.

ADVISE

Closed handshape on back of left hand opens and moves forward.

Can also mean—Counsel

AFRAID

Move both hands toward center of chest. Repeat motion.

Can also mean—Scared, fearful

AFTER

Slide upright hand over back of left hand.

AFTERNOON

Elbow of right forearm rests on back of left hand; right hand waves down. Repeat motion.

AGAIN

Bent fingers arc onto palm of other hand.

Can also mean—Repeat

AGAINST

Straight fingers of right hand move in straight line into palm of left hand.

Can also mean—Oppose

AGGRESSIVE

Hands move out and back in alternating circles, brushing body on inward movements.

AGREE

Right index finger touches side of head, then moves down to rest parallel to left index finger.

AHEAD

With thumbs stretched upward, right hand arcs over and stops in front of left hand.

AIRPLANE

Stretch out index finger, little finger, and thumb; move hand through air, right to left. Repeat motion.

ALARM

Index finger taps twice against left palm.

ALCOHOL

Stretch out index finger and little finger and bring hand down onto identical left handshape. Repeat motion.

Can also mean—Liquor

ALL

Right hand sweeps in front, around, and behind left hand, and turns to rest in left palm.

ALL OVER

Open hand with five fingers spread; sweep in wide counterclockwise arc.

Can also mean—Everywhere

ALL RIGHT

Flat upright hand slides up and forward across left palm before being lifted upward. Repeat motion.

Can also mean—Okay, fine

ALLERGY

Touch tip of nose with index finger, bring both index fingers together, and then draw them apart.

ALLOW

Parallel hands sweep up and forward.

Can also mean—Permit

ALMOST

Fingers of bent right hand move up the tips of back of bent left-hand fingers.

Can also mean—Nearly

ALONE

Forearm with extended index finger describes two small, counterclockwise circles from elbow.

Can also mean—Single

ALTERNATE

"L" handshape sweeps in an arc to left side and back.

ALWAYS

Forearm with extended index finger describes two large, counterclockwise circles from elbow.

AMAZED

Two fists open quickly into claw shapes and close again.

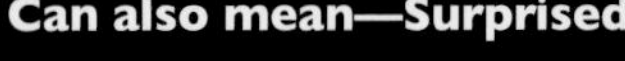

Can also mean—Surprised

AMBULANCE

Outstretched fingers rotate back and forth at either side of head.

ANALYZE

"V" handshapes move down while crooking fingers twice.

AND

Open hand closes as it moves right across body.

ANGRY

Claw hand in front of body arcs up and out past face.

Can also mean—Mad (with rage)

ANNOUNCE

Touch index fingers to chin and sweep them out and away from each other.

ANSWER

Index fingers, right at chin, left in front, move down and forward.

Can also mean—Respond, reply

ANXIOUS

Bend middle fingers and alternately touch chest, then swing out and back in small arcs.

Can also mean—Nervous, concerned, worried

ANY

Clench fist with thumb stretched out and rotate hand in front of body.

ANYONE

Clench fist with thumb outstretched, turn hand down and then up; hide thumb and point index finger upward.

ANYWAY

With fingers together, thumbs outstretched, alternately bring hands toward and away from body, fingertips touching as they pass.

APPEAR (SHOW UP)

Index finger rises up between index and middle fingers of left hand.

APPLAUD

Clap hands together. Repeat motion quickly.

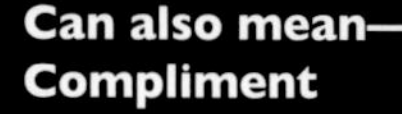
Can also mean—
Compliment

APPLE

Crook index finger and rotate against cheek. Repeat motion.

APPLY

With thumb and index finger, pull shirt slightly out and back twice.

APPOINTMENT

Rotate open hand; close to "A" handshape and place on back of other hand.

APPROVE

"A" handshape changes to "K" handshape as it stamps against left palm.

APPROXIMATELY

Open hand, palm out, and rotate slowly counterclockwise.

Can also mean—About (roughly)

AREA

Open hand, palm down, describes a couple of counterclockwise circles.

ARRIVE

Back of right hand lands in palm of left.

ART

Little finger moves down palm with curving motion.

ARTICLE

Thumb and bent index finger move down palm.

ASHAMED

Wipe back of fingers against cheek and bring hand forward and down.

ASK

Straight index finger bends and moves out and down.

Can also mean—Inquire, question

ASSIGN

Fork index and middle fingers over index finger of other hand.

ASSISTANT

Clench fists and outstretch thumbs; tap thumb against base of left fist twice.

ATTEND

Outstretch index fingers and point hands down and forward. Repeat motion.

ATTITUDE

The "A" handshape circles and the back of the thumb lands at the opposite shoulder.

ATTRACTED TO

Open hand in front of face moves down and forward to clenched fist.

Can also mean—
Fascinated

AUDIENCE

Outstretch hands close together in front of body, then bring back toward shoulders as fingers bend.

AUNT

Place "A" handshape at side of chin and rock slightly.

AVERAGE

Tap vertical hand twice against horizontal left hand so that little finger hits at middle.

Can also mean—Medium

AVOID

With thumbs up, move back hand away from front left hand.

AWKWARD

Stretch out thumb, index, and middle fingers and then alternately move each hand up and down in front of body.

Can also mean—Clumsy

BABY

With one flat hand atop the other, mime rocking a baby.

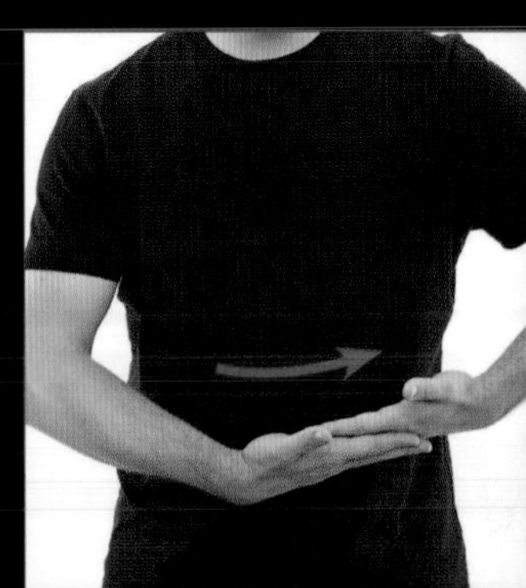

BACON

Index and middle fingers move away and up and down, miming the shape of a strip of bacon.

BAD

Place fingertips to lips and then move hand down with palm facing downward.

BAKE

Mime placing object in oven; lower hand, palm up, slides forward under left hand.

BALANCE

Bent hands alternately move up and down.

BALL

Fingers of both hands touch twice in shape of ball.

BANANA

Mime peeling banana skin, using index finger as banana.

BANK

"B" handshape moves down and back up quickly to "K" handshape.

BASEBALL

Imitate holding baseball bat and move slightly forward twice.

BASEMENT

Circle right fist with thumb extended under left palm twice.

Can also mean—Cellar

BASIC

Circle right hand under left palm twice.

BASKETBALL

Mime swiveling basketball between thumb, index, and middle fingers. Repeat motion.

BEACH

Right hand opens across left forearm. Repeat.

BEAR (ANIMAL)

Cross arms and scratch shoulders with claw hands in small circles.

BECAUSE

Touch forehead with index finger, then move hand away from head, thumb in air.

Can also mean—Since (time)

BECOME

Cross palms together in front of body; reverse position of hands in a sweep across chest, keeping palms together.

BED

Lean head to side and tap twice with palm of hand.

BEER

Brush side of cheek twice with fingers, palm facing out.

BEFORE

Right hand moves back toward shoulder from behind left hand.

Can also mean—Former, past

BELIEVE

Touch head with index finger and lower hand to clasp left palm.

BELL

Closed right hand taps twice against upright palm of left hand like a bell clapper.

BELOW

With fingers bent, meet fingertips in front of body and move right hand down.

Can also mean—Less than

BENEFIT

Thumb and index finger strike chest gently while hand moves downward from wrist.

BEST

Raise fingers toward mouth and move hand up and out to side of head while making fist, keeping thumb extended.

BET

Place hands, palms facing, in front of body and lower, palms down, as though covering cards.

BETTER

Raise fingers toward mouth and move hand out to side of head while making a fist, keeping thumb extended.

BETWEEN

Slide upright hand back and forth twice between thumb and index finger of left hand.

BICYCLE

Clench fists and imitate forward pedaling motion.

BIG

Thumb and bent index finger handshapes face each other and are then drawn apart.

Can also mean—Large

BIOLOGY

"B" handshapes describe alternating circles on a vertical plane.

BIRD

Thumb and index finger close twice at mouth.

BIRTHDAY

Touch bent middle finger to chin and then to center of chest.

BLIND

Move bent index and middle fingers in toward eyes.

BLONDE

"Y" handshape moves away and turns out from side of head.

BLOOD

Fingers of right hand wiggle as the hand moves down from under left. Repeat.

BOAST

Alternately bring thumbs in to touch waist and out again.

Can also mean—Brag

BOAT

Cup hands together; move down and forward and back up again, then end with hands down and forward.

Can also mean—Ship

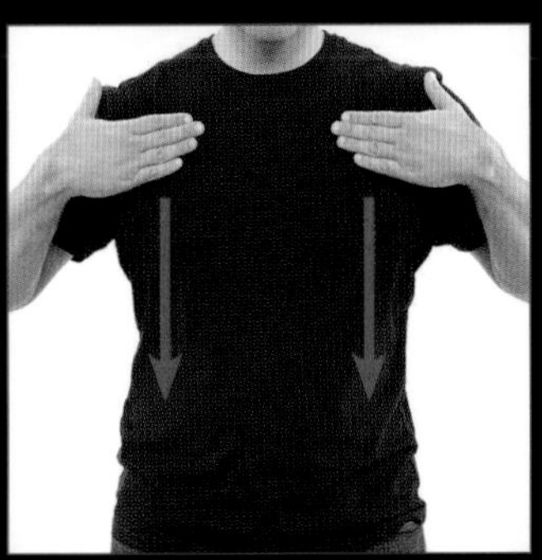
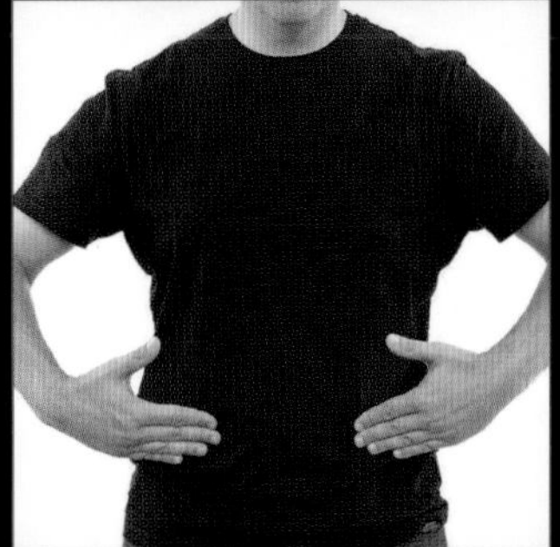

BODY

Place hands on chest near shoulders; bring both hands down to the waist.

BOOK

Place palms together, then imitate opening and closing book. Repeat motion.

BORING

Twist index finger at side of nose.

BORN

Slide lower hand forward underneath the palm of the upper hand.

Can also mean—Birth

BORROW

With right "V" handshape on left, move hands back toward body.

Can also mean—Lend

BOSS

With hand in a claw shape, tap shoulder with fingertips twice.

Can also mean—Captain

BOTH

Make fork shape with middle and index fingers and draw through left hand, from top to bottom, while closing fingers.

BOTHER

Using chopping motion, strike other hand between thumb and index finger twice.

BOWLING

Imitate grasping ball in hand; swing arm back and forth twice.

BOY

Touch thumb to fingertips at forehead twice.

Can also mean—Male

BRAVE

Place claw hands on front of shoulders, then bring hands out to form fists.

Can also mean—Confident, healthy

BREAD

Bent hand moves along back of other hand with short downward movements.

BREAK (DAMAGE)

Touch sides of fists together, then separate; finish with knuckles facing each other.

BREAKFAST

Bring right fingertips to lips, then open out arm in front of body; touch inside of right elbow with left hand, then raise right hand to side of face.

BREATHE

Place right hand on chest and left on abdomen; lift hands away from body and back in again.

BRIDGE

Touch index and middle fingers to wrist and move in an arc to touch elbow.

BRING

Mime lifting an object from one side of body in toward the body.

Can also mean—Carry

BROKE (NO MONEY)

Using chopping motion, tap side of neck with hand.

BROTHER

Touch thumb of "L" handshape against forehead and swing down to rest on top of left hand.

BUG (INSECT)

Touch nose with thumb, with middle and index fingers outstretched; then crook middle and index fingers twice.

BUILD

Move hands up and down in front of body so that tips of index and middle fingers touch as they pass. Repeat.

BULLETIN BOARD

Mime sticking up a poster; press thumbs slightly forward at top and bottom.

BURY

"U" handshape moves down past left hand.

BUSY

"B" handshape moves back and forth along back of left wrist. Repeat motion.

BUT

Cross index fingers in front of chest and move outward.

BUTTER

Stroke index and middle fingers inward twice on left palm.

BUY

Closed hand moves outward from left palm and opens.

C

CAKE

Clawed right hand comes down on left palm and rises back up.

CALL (SUMMON)

In one motion, right hand taps back of left hand and pulls back to "A" handshape.

CAMERA

Mime taking a photo, using index finger to click shutter.

CAMP

Bring tips of little and index fingers together; move hands apart and downward. Repeat.

CAN (ABLE)

Fists at shoulder level, move down in front of body.

CAN'T

Index finger strikes down across left index finger.

Can also mean—Unable

CANCEL

Using index finger, draw a large "X" on left palm.

CANDLE

Touch index finger to wrist of upright right hand and wiggle fingers of right hand.

CANDY

Touch index finger to cheek and rotate finger forward, back, and forward again.

CAPTION

Meet "F" handshapes at thumbs and index fingers and pull apart. Repeat motion.

CAR

Close both hands into fists and mime steering a wheel.

Can also mean— Automobile

CAREFUL

Place right "V" handshape on top of left "V" handshape and circle forward twice.

CAREFUL (BE)

"V" handshape taps twice on left "V" handshape.

Can also mean—Cautious

CARELESS

"V" handshapes swing down across front of face and back again.

CAT

Bring thumb and index finger of both hands together in front of cheeks and mime stroking a whisker twice.

CATCH UP

Right fist with thumb extended moves forward to butt against left hand.

CAUSE (VERB)

With left fist behind right fist, separate hands, stretch fingers, and move hands outward.

CELEBRATE

Crook index fingers and rotate both hands at side of head.

CELL PHONE

Mime holding a cell phone and touch fingers to cheek twice.

CENT

Index finger touches side of forehead and pulls away.

CERTIFICATE

Tap thumbs of "C" handshapes together twice.

CHAIR

Curved index and middle fingers move down twice onto straight index and middle fingers of left hand.

CHALLENGE

Fists with thumbs extended swing up to meet at knuckles.

Can also mean—Dare

CHAMPION

Bring palm of claw hand onto tip of left index finger and pull up again.

CHANGE (MODIFY)

Bring "X" handshapes together, right on left, and turn over to reverse positions.

CHARACTER (PERSONAL)

"C" handshape makes small counterclockwise circle and ends on shoulder.

CHARGE (PURCHASE)

Slide fist along left palm, from fingertips to wrist, and back out again.

Can also mean—Credit card

CHASE

Stick both thumbs up and rotate back right hand in repeated sideways circles.

Can also mean—Pursue

CHAT

Move open handshapes back and forth in front of shoulders a few times.

CHEAP

Strike left hand a downward glancing blow.

CHEAT

Fork middle and index finger over fingers of other hand twice.

CHEERFUL

Spread hands and wiggle fingers at either side of face as hands move up. Repeat motion.

Can also mean—Friendly, pleasant

CHEESE

Join hands at base of palms; swivel through an arc of 45 degrees back and forth.

CHEMISTRY

"C" handshapes move alternately in vertical in-and-out circles.

CHERISH

Claw hand closes to fist on point of chin.

CHICKEN

Join thumb and index finger to form beak that closes twice on left palm.

CHILD

Bent hand moves down twice as if on child's head.

CHILDREN

With hands flat, palms down, make patting motion in center, side, and farther out from body.

CHOCOLATE

Move thumb of "C" handshape in a circular motion on back of left hand.

CHOOSE

Using thumb and index finger, mime picking something from tip of index finger on other hand.

CHURCH

Back of right "C" handshape thumb taps back of left hand twice.

CIGARETTE

Tips of index and little fingers touch side of left index finger twice.

CITY

Form inverted "V" by tapping fingertips together twice.

Can also mean—Town

CLASS

Move "C" handshapes down and away from chest in an arc to finish with palms facing inward.

CLEAN (ADJECTIVE)

Wipe inside of fingers against palm of other hand, from base of palm to fingertips.

Can also mean—Neat (tidy)

CLEAN UP (VERB)

Slide inside of fingers twice along palm of other hand, from base of palm to fingertips.

CLEAR

Bring thumbs and fingertips together in front of chest; draw hands up and away, spreading fingers, palms out.

Can also mean—Obvious

CLOSE (VERB)

Fold thumbs in, hands at either side of shoulders; bring together in center so that palms face out.

CLOSET

Cross inside of index and middle fingers; tap against each other, then reverse position, top to bottom.

CLOTHES

Brush thumb tips of open hands down chest twice.

CLOUDS

Using claw handshapes, right palm down and left up, rotate around each other while moving across body.

COFFEE

Place right fist on top of left fist and move in circles to mime grinding.

COLD (TEMPERATURE)

Hunch shoulders and make shivering motion with fists.

COLD (ILLNESS)

Curl fingers in and pull hand down twice over nose, between index finger and outstretched thumb.

COLLEGE

Slide right palm right, forward, and up to the left over left palm.

COLOR

Wiggle fingertips against chin.

COMB

Mime combing hair, using bent fingertips as teeth of comb.

COME

Point index fingers out and then in.

COMFORTABLE

Rub palm of right hand across and down back of left hand; reverse hands and repeat.

COMMAND

Place side of index finger on chin and move sideways in one motion and point outward in front of body.

Can also mean—Order

COMMUNICATE

Alternately move "C" handshapes in and away from chin.

COMMUTE

With thumb up, move hand diagonally out from shoulder and back again twice.

COMPARE

Place hands out at either side of head, with one palm facing in and the other out; alternately orbit hands in and away from face.

COMPETE

Touch knuckles of fists together, with thumbs extended; alternately point thumbs toward and away from chest.

Can also mean—Race

COMPLAIN

Tap claw handshape against middle of chest twice.

COMPLICATED

Point index fingers up; alternately crook and straighten index fingers while moving hands across each other.

COMPUTER

Move "C" handshape along back of left forearm twice.

CONFLICT

Bring hands together at bases of outstretched index fingers.

CONFUSED

Touch head with index finger and rotate claw handshapes around each other, right over left.

CONGRATULATE

Clasp hands together and shake backward and forward twice in front of body.

CONNECT

Bring hands together, locking thumbs and index fingers around each other.

CONTACT

Bring tips of middle fingers together.

CONTINUE

Press right thumb on left and move hands forward in front of chest.

CONTROL

Crook index fingers and alternately move hands in and away from body.

Can also mean—Manage

COOK

Touch palm of right hand to palm of left hand, then flip right hand over and touch back of right hand against palm of left hand. Repeat.

COOKIE

Mime using a cookie cutter on palm of other hand.

COOL (GOOD)

Touch thumb to center of chest and wiggle other fingers.

COOL (TEMPERATURE)

Flap fingers toward face.

COOPERATE

Lock thumbs and index fingers together and rotate hands horizontally in front of chest.

COPY

Open right hand moves back in and closes to rest with fingertips on left palm.

CORNER

Place hands at right angles and bring together; tap fingertips together twice.

COST

Crook index finger and slide down left palm.

Can also mean—Price

COUGH

Tap center of chest with clenched fist twice.

COUNTRY

Use inside of hand to make circular motions on opposite elbow.

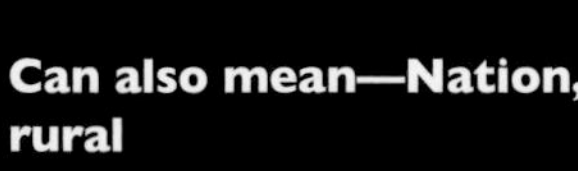
Can also mean—Nation, rural

COUSIN

Using "C" handshape, swivel hand twice next to head.

COW

Touch thumbs to side of head, little fingers pointing up; twist hands down and back twice.

CRAVE

With palm out and thumb folded in, draw index finger down cheek, from above to below lips.

Can also mean—Desire

CRAZY

Point index finger and draw circles at side of head.

CREATE

Fold thumb in and touch side of forehead with tip of index finger; lift hand up and away.

Can also mean—Invent

CRITICIZE

Using index finger, draw small "X" on left palm.

CROSS (OVER)

Sweep upright hand over wrist of left hand, moving in an arc from back to front.

CROWDED

With palms together and fingers outstretched, turn hands around while keeping them pressed together.

CRY

Touch index fingers to cheeks below eyes; bend index fingers and bring hands down. Repeat motion.

CURIOUS

Touch thumb and index finger to throat and shake hand slightly.

CUTE

Touch index and middle fingers to chin; move down and close into hand.

DANCE

Swing forked index and middle finger over other palm.

DANGEROUS

With thumbs pointing upward and fists clenched, swing outer hand up and bounce knuckles on back of other hand. Repeat motion.

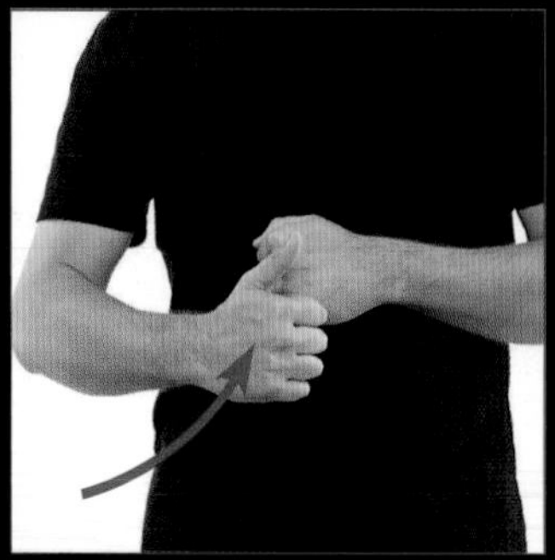

DARK

With palms facing in, cross hands in front of face.

DAY

Position arms at right angles; stretch out index finger of vertical right arm and swing down to rest on left elbow.

DEAD

With one palm up and one palm down, rotate hands 180 degrees to reverse position.

Can also mean—Die

DEAF

Touch index finger to ear and then to side of chin.

DECEIVE

Tap folded knuckles of "A" handshape against upright left index finger and pull away.

Can also mean—Trick

DECIDE

Touch index finger to side of head and bring hand down even with other hand, both hands ending side by side in "F" handshapes.

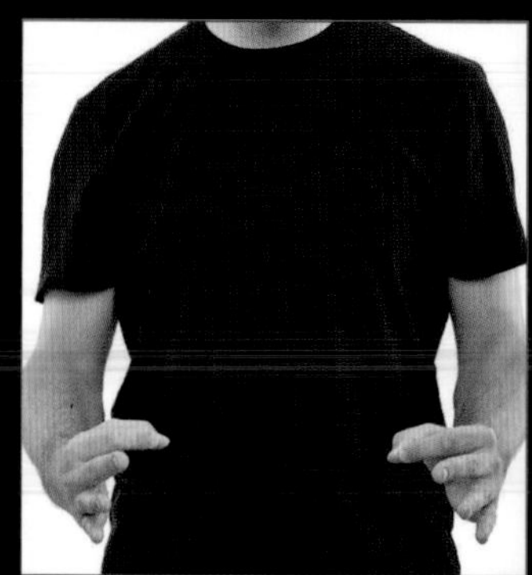

DECLINE

Right index finger touches side of chin and then hand moves down so that fingertips slide out along left palm.

DECREASE

Right "U" handshape turns over and moves down off left "U" handshape.

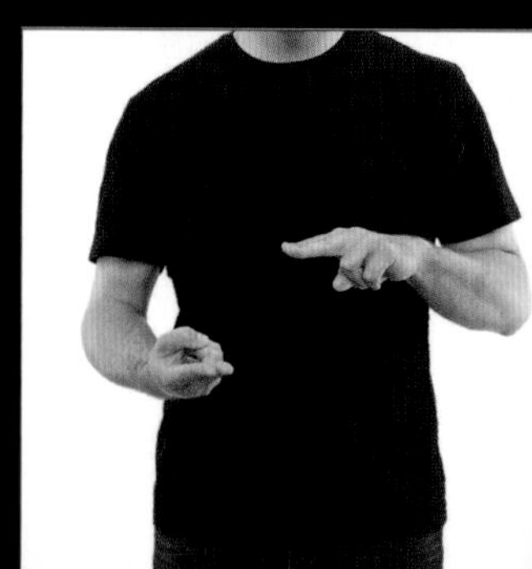

DEEP

Bring down pointing index finger past horizontal left hand.

DEFEAT

Clench fists and bend right wrist over the left.

Can also mean—Beat

DELETE

Tuck thumb tip under tip of index finger; flick thumb up and out while moving hand up and out.

DELICIOUS

Join thumb and middle finger below mouth; bring hand down and slide middle finger back along underside of thumb.

DEMOTED

Lower bent hands from shoulder height.

DENTIST

Crooked index finger taps corner of mouth twice.

DEODORANT

With "X" handshape, mime spraying deodorant under left arm.

DEPART

Bring hands up and across body while closing fingers.

Can also mean—Go, leave

DEPEND ON

Right index fingertip pushes down on left index fingertip twice.

Can also mean—Rely on

DEPRESSED

Open hands and touch middle fingers to either side of chest; slide hands down body.

DESPERATE

Alternately rotate middle fingers in to touch chin in downward circles.

DESTROY

Place right hand above left, palms facing, and move right hand back over left while closing both hands to "A" handshapes.

Can also mean—Damage, ruin

DETERIORATE

Begin with thumbs up at shoulder level; wiggle hands while bringing hands down in front of body.

DICTIONARY

Strike palm two glancing blows with a "D" handshape.

DIFFERENT

Cross index fingers and pull them out and apart.

DIFFICULT

Bend index and middle fingers of both hands; strike side of right hand against side of left.

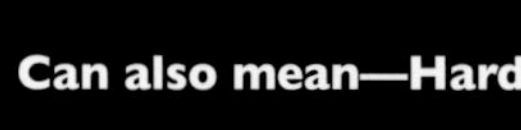
Can also mean—Hard

DINNER

Place fingers to mouth; bring hand down and curve over wrist of other arm.

DIPLOMA

Touch thumbs and index fingers of "F" handshapes together, then pull apart.

DIRTY

Place back of hand under chin and wiggle fingers.

DISAGREE

Touch index finger to side of head; bring both index fingers together and then pull apart.

DISAPPEAR

Point index finger up between index and middle finger of left hand; bring pointing index finger down and bend finger.

DISCONNECT

Lock thumbs and index fingers together; break chain and separate hands.

DISCUSS

Tap side of index finger on left palm a few times.

Can also mean—Debate

DISTRIBUTE

Closed hands meet at fingertips; hands spread open while moving out and forward.

DIVIDE (MATH)

Edge of right hand touches left, then hands separate out and down.

DIVORCE

Clasped hands, right on left, separate out and down, both ending in "C" handshapes.

DOCTOR

Tap fingertips against inside of left wrist twice.

DOG

Slap thigh and bring hand up to snap fingers.

DOLLAR

Clasp left palm between heel and fingers of right hand and slide right hand along past left fingertips. Repeat motion.

DON'T

Cross hands at wrists and move apart.

DON'T CARE

Touch closed fingers to nose; turn hand away and stretch fingers out in a flicking motion.

DOOR

Fold thumbs in and place hands together in upright position, palms out; move right hand away while twisting palm in. Repeat motion.

DOUBT (UNSURE)

Clench fists and alternately move forearms and fists up and down. Repeat motion.

DREAM

Touch index finger to side of head; crook index finger while moving hand up and away from head.

DRINK

With "C" handshape, mime sipping from a glass.

DRIVE A CAR

Move fists together away from body twice.

DROP

Hold fists at chest level; drop hands down while stretching out fingers.

DROWN

Extend thumb of fist; move down between index and middle fingers of left hand.

DRY

Index finger moves from left corner of mouth across chin to right corner, ending in "X" handshape.

DURING

Move parallel index fingers forward in a slight down/ up arc.

Can also mean—While

DUTY

Tap joined index and middle fingers of "D" handshape twice on left wrist.

EACH

With thumbs up, slide right knuckles down base of left thumb.

Can also mean—Every

EARLY

Touch middle finger to back of left hand; bend finger and move hand forward and down.

EARN

Cup hand but keep thumb up; draw hand over palm while closing fingers.

Can also mean—Collect

EARRINGS

Place tips of thumbs behind earlobes and tips of index fingers on top of earlobes; shake gently twice.

EARTH

Use thumb and middle finger to clasp left hand; rock right hand, left and right.

EAST

"E" handshape moves to the right.

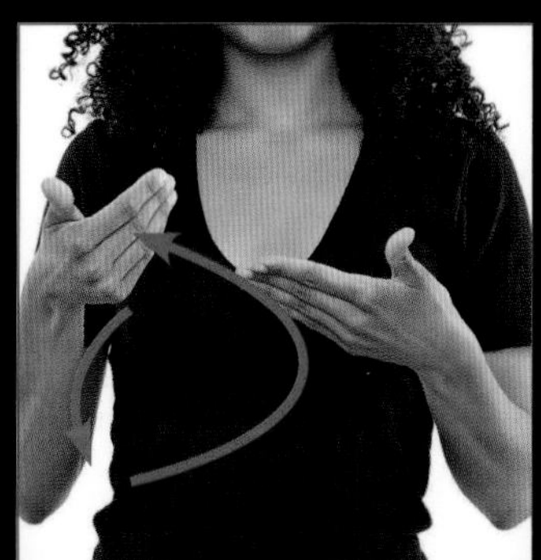

EASY

Fingertips of right hand slap fingertips of left hand twice as they pass by.

EAT

Tap mouth twice with fingertips.

ECSTATIC

Index and middle fingers of right hand jump up and bend from left palm. Repeat motion.

Can also mean—Delighted

EGG

Index and middle fingers of right hand slide over the index and middle fingers of the left, then move down and away. Repeat motion.

EGOTISTICAL

Thumbs and bent index fingers move out sideways from either side of head.

Can also mean—Conceited

EITHER

Wiggle tips of index and middle fingers onto same fingers of left hand.

ELECTION

Thumb and index finger mime placing something into top of other clenched hand twice.

ELECTRICITY

Bring knuckles of "X" handshapes together twice.

ELEPHANT

Imitate elephant trunk by placing upright hand in front of nose, then sweeping hand down and out.

ELEVATOR

"E" handshape slides up and down left palm.

EMBARRASSED

Fingers outstretched, palms in; alternately move hands up and down at side of face in slightly circular movements.

EMERGENCY

"E" handshape shakes back and forth a few times.

EMOTIONAL

"E" handshapes alternately rotate outward in front of chest.

EMPTY

Middle finger slides across back of other hand, from wrist outward.

ENCOURAGE

Move open hands forward while rotating them in small outward circles.

END

Right fingertips slide down in front of left fingertips at right angle.

ENGAGED (BETROTHED)

"E" handshape makes a small circle down onto back of left ring finger.

ENJOY

Rotate both hands against the body, right above left, in opposite circles.

Can also mean—
Appreciate

ENOUGH

Palm of right hand moves forward twice across top of left fist.

ENTER

Right hand, palm down, slides forward under left.

ENTHUSIASTIC

Rub hands together.

Can also mean—Eager

EQUAL

Bend fingers and bring tips of both hands together and touch twice.

ESCAPE

Slide right index finger outward between index and middle fingers of left hand.

ESTABLISH

Fist with thumb extended swings up and then down onto back of left hand.

EXACT

Place tips of index fingers and thumbs together; rotate right hand and bring down on same joined tips of left hand.

EXAGGERATE

Place right fist in front of left; bring right fist away from body in an up/down arc.

EXCITED

Point middle fingers in; alternately rotate hands in toward chest, middle fingers touching chest as they pass.

EXCUSE

Right fingertips slide out along left palm.

Can also mean—Forgive

EXCUSE ME

Slide fingertips along left palm twice in short movements.

EXERCISE (PHYSICAL)

Raise fists up from shoulders twice.

EXPAND

Place right fist on top of left fist; draw hands apart and stretch out fingers.

EXPECT

Bend fingers up and down twice, with one hand held higher.

Can also mean—Hope

EXPENSIVE

Fingertips move up from left palm, then flick open and down.

EXPERIENCE

Fingertips close while sliding down cheek. Repeat motion.

EXPERT

Place tip of index finger and thumb together; bring up to chin.

EXPLAIN

Place tips of index fingers and thumbs together; alternately move hands toward and away from body.

Can also mean—Describe

EXPRESS

Place fists near each other close to body, then move hands forward, palms up, while stretching open fingers.

EYES

Touch index finger to face below right eye and then again below the left.

FACE

Encircle face using index finger.

FAIL

“V” handshape slides down and off left palm.

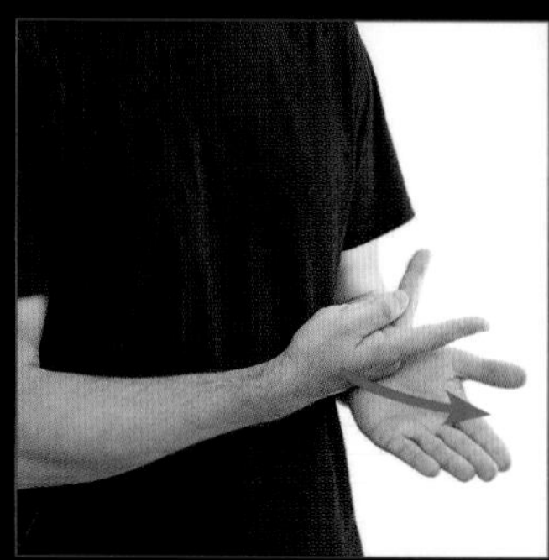

FAINT

Touch forehead with index finger; bring other hand up and sweep hands away to form fists at side of body.

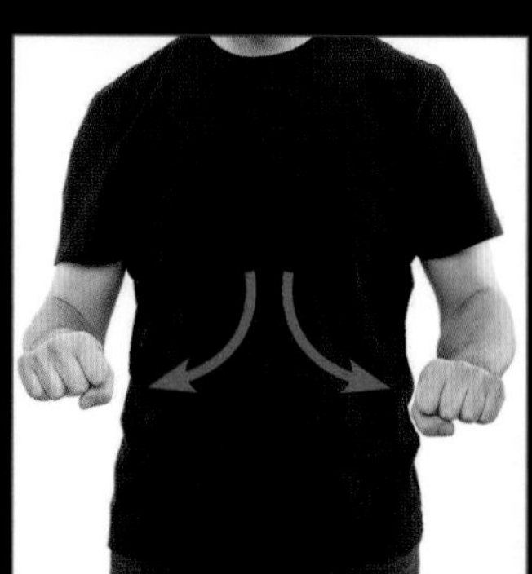

FALL ASLEEP

Touch forehead with index finger, then extend all fingers out and bring hand down to meet other hand, palms in; close eyes and lower head.

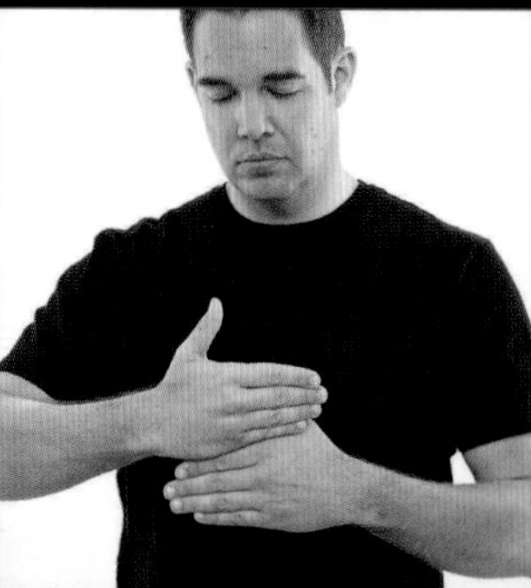

FALL BEHIND

Right hand, thumb extended, moves back from left hand toward body.

FALL DOWN

Stand index and middle fingers on left palm; move fingers upward and collapse back of hand onto left palm.

FALL IN LOVE

Touch index finger between eyes; bring hand down on left palm and bounce forward to fingertips.

FAMILY

"F" handshapes touch at thumbs and index fingers, then swing out, around, and back together.

FAMOUS

Touch index fingers at either side of chin; bring hands away from chin in two small arcs.

FANTASY

"F" handshapes rotate alternately at either side of head.

FAR

Point index finger up and move hand away.

Can also mean—Distant

FARM

Stretch out fingers and slide thumb from left side of chin to the right.

FAST (SPEED)

Stretch fingers out in front of body, left hand farther forward; draw both hands back quickly and clench fists.

Can also mean—Quick

FAT

Point hands to either side of waist; bring hands out.

FATHER

Tap thumb of open hand on forehead twice.

FAULT (NOUN)

Place fingertips on shoulder and hinge hand downward, keeping fingers where they are.

FAVORITE

Tap middle finger on chin twice.

Can also mean—Prefer

FED UP

Raise fingers of back of hand to underside of chin.

FEED

Bring fingertips together on both hands, then push hands forward twice, right hand in front.

FEEL

Touch middle finger to center of chest and slide upward.

FEW

"A" handshape, palm up, spreads partially open.

FIGHT

Clench fists and cross arms.

FIGURE OUT

"V" handshapes cross at wrists. Repeat motion.

FIND

Mime picking something up between thumb and index finger.

Can also mean—Discover

FINE

Tap center of chest twice with thumb.

Can also mean—OK

FINISH

Stretch fingers out, palms facing in, then sweep hands around so that palms now face out.

Can also mean—Already

FIRE (FLAME)

Stretch fingers out, palms in; alternately move hands up and down in front of chest while wiggling fingers.

Can also mean—Burn

FIRE (FROM JOB)

Swipe back of hand across top of left fist.

FIRST

Right index finger moves in to touch extended left thumb.

FISH

Move upright hand forward and across body while making wavy motions.

FISHING

Both hands have crooked index fingers touching thumb tips; with left hand in front, flick hands forward twice, as if casting a fishing line.

FIX

Fold fingers over thumbs; point both hands together and alternately move toward and away from body twice so that fingertips touch while crossing.

Can also mean—Repair

FLAG

Touch left index finger to wrist of right hand; flap right hand like a flag waving in the breeze.

FLATTER

Point left index finger up; swipe fingers of right hand back and forth over the pointing finger.

FLEXIBLE

Clasp fingers of left hand between thumb and index finger of right hand; move hand backward and forward, bending left hand to show flexibility.

FLIRT

Join thumbs together and bring hands in and out while wiggling fingers.

FLOWER

Bring fingertips together and move hand in an arc from one side of nose to other.

FOLLOW (TRAIL)

Place right hand behind left and move both forward.

FOOTBALL

Bring hands together so that fingers interlock; repeat motion.

FOR

Index finger touches side of head and twists forward and out.

FORBIDDEN

Slap "L" handshape against left palm and pull away quickly.

Can also mean—Illegal

FORCE (VERB)

Bend "C" handshape over left wrist.

FOREIGN

"F" handshape rotates on opposite elbow.

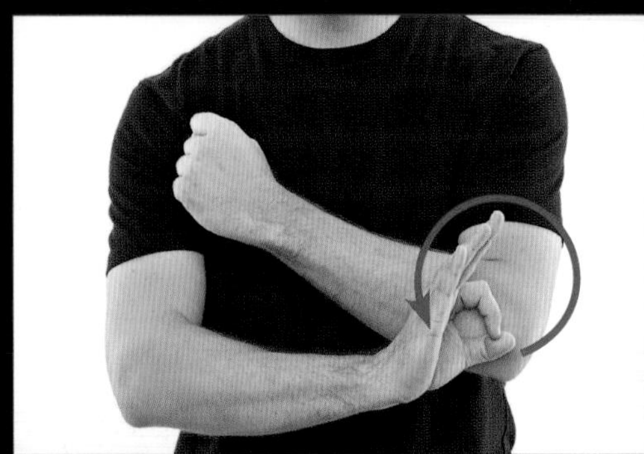

FOREVER

Index finger touches side of forehead, then becomes "Y" handshape, turns, and moves forward.

FORGET

Move fingertips across forehead from left to right, then close.

FORK

Tap index and middle fingers into palm twice.

FREE

"F" handshapes cross, palms in, then separate and open outward.

FREEZE

Stretch out hands, palms down; claw fingers in while bringing hands toward chest.

FROM

Hold left index finger vertically; crook right index finger and bring in toward body.

FRONT

Move palm down in front of face.

FRUIT

"F" handshape twists forward and backward on cheek.

FULL

Swipe palm back and to the left over left fist.

Can also mean—Fill

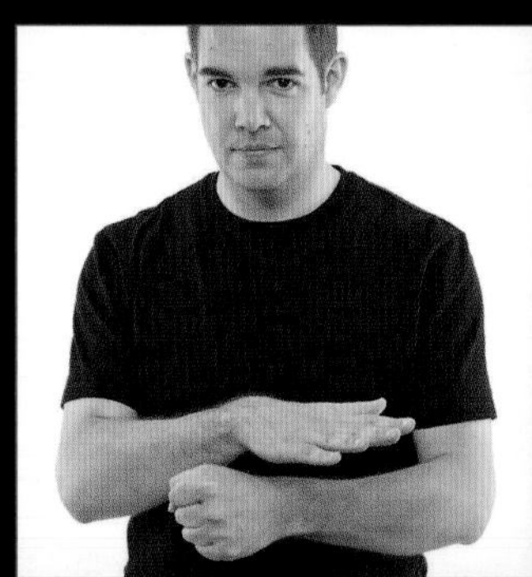

FUN

Touch nose with index and middle fingers, then swoop them down onto the same fingers on left hand.

FUNNY

Flick index and middle fingers on the end of the nose twice.

FUTURE

Palm moves forward from beside right cheek.

Can also mean—Will

G

GAME

Raise thumbs and bring knuckles together twice.

Can also mean—Sports

GARAGE

Stretch out thumb, index, and middle fingers; move hand back and forth under left palm.

GENERAL

Bring tips of fingers together in "V" shape, palms in; flap hands apart, palms out.

Can also mean—Broad

GET (ACQUIRE)

Bring open hands toward body while closing into fists, right above left.

Can also mean—Acquire, obtain, receive, procure

GET IN

Bend index and middle fingers; move onto thumb of left "C" handshape.

GET ON

Fork index and middle fingers and wedge up and over fingers of left hand.

GIRL

Brush side of jaw with inside of thumb twice.

Can also mean—Female

GIVE

Closed handshape moves up, forward, and down.

GIVE IN

Place palm against chest; bring hand out, palm facing up.

Can also mean—Concede, admit

GLASS (CUP)

"C" handshape comes down on left palm twice.

GLASS (MATERIAL)

Crook index finger and tap chin twice.

Can also mean—Finland

GLASSES

With index fingers crooked, thumb tips tap cheeks twice below eyes, miming adjusting spectacles.

GO

Index fingers move forward and decline to horizontal.

GOD

Flat hand moves down to rest vertically near chin.

GOOD

Fingertips move down and forward from chin.

GOSSIP

Open and close thumbs and index fingers while moving hands in counterclockwise horizontal circles from mouth.

Can also mean—Rumor

G

GOVERNMENT

Index finger bends, turns toward head, and straightens against temple.

GRANDFATHER

Thumb of open hand touches forehead and moves down and out in two small arcs.

GRANDMOTHER

Thumb of open hand touches chin and moves down and out in two small arcs.

GRIEF

Bring fists together near heart and wring one hand down, one hand up in a twisting motion.

Can also mean—Agony, misery

GROUP

Open claw hands to circle around invisible ball.

GROW

Closed right hand moves up and opens from inside cupped left hand.

GROW UP

Horizontal hand moves up to head.

GUILTY

Index handshape taps left shoulder twice.

H

HABIT

Right hand crosses onto left at wrist; hands lower and close to fists.

Can also mean—Tendency

HAIR

Thumb and index finger move out from side of head twice.

HAMBURGER

Clasp hands; swap position of hands and clasp again.

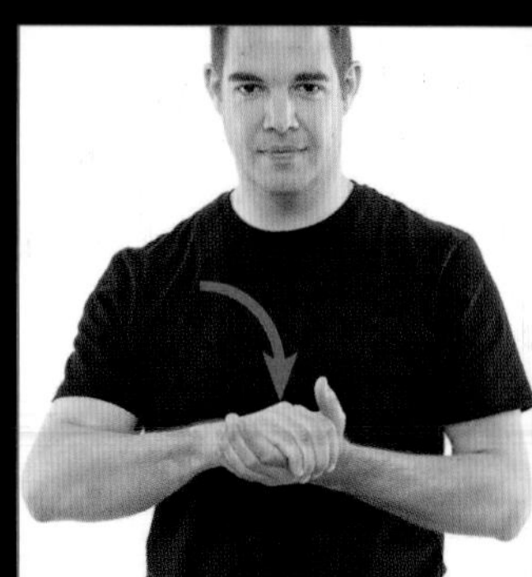

HANDS

Slide edge of right hand in across wrist of left hand and repeat action with hands reversed.

HANDSOME

Move hand outward from chin, then describe a circle around face.

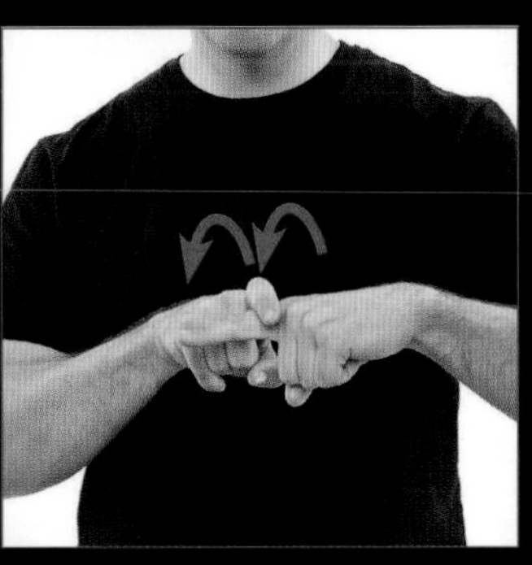

HANGER (CLOTHES)

Hooked right index finger bounces twice, left to right, along left index finger.

HAPPEN

Palms up, point index fingers and raise hands; lower hands while turning palms down.

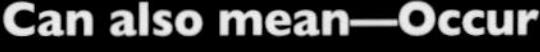

Can also mean—Occur

HAPPY

Hand describes two upward and outward circles, touching chest as it passes.

Can also mean—Pleased, lighthearted, contented, glad

HARD (SOLID)

Raise fists and bring knuckles down on back of left hand twice.

Can also mean—Solid

HARD OF HEARING

"H" handshape moves down and bounces once to the right.

HAT

Pat top of head twice.

HATE

Flick middle fingers out from thumbs.

HAVE

Bent hands move in to touch either side of chest with fingertips.

Can also mean—Possess, own

HE

Point with index finger.

Can also mean—She, it, there

HEAD

Fingertips of bent hand touch side of head and then side of chin.

HEAR

Touch ear with index finger.

HEARING AID

Hook index finger around ear and tap down twice.

HEART

Tap twice at heart with middle finger.

HELLO

Hand moves out from forehead.

HELP

Place right fist, thumb up, on left palm and raise both hands.

HERE

Place hands, palms up, at either side of body; bring hands in and out using a circular motion.

HIDE

Back of thumb moves down from mouth to hide under left palm.

HIGH

"H" handshape moves up at side of body.

HIGH SCHOOL

Make the "H" and "S" handshapes.

HIGHWAY

Point index and middle fingers across body and then move hands back and forth past each other twice.

HIRE

With palm up, bring hand in toward center of body.

Can also mean—Invite

HIS

Move hand in direction of person.

Can also mean—Her

HISTORY

Move "H" handshape up and down twice.

HOCKEY

Sweep knuckle of crooked index finger down onto palm of other hand. Repeat motion.

HOLD

Clench fist and shake hand in front of shoulder.

HOLY

"H" handshape moves to base of palm of upturned left hand, turns over and changes to flat hand, and slides out across left palm.

HOME

Closed fingers touch side of lower and then upper cheek.

HONEST

Middle finger of "H" handshape slides out along left palm.

Can also mean—Truth

HONOR

Start with "H" handshapes; right hand on forehead, left hand in front and below. Bring hands down and out from body.

HORSE

Touch thumbs of "H" handshapes to side of head and bend index and middle fingers down twice.

HOSPITAL

Fingers of "H" handshape draw cross on side of left shoulder.

HOT

Claw handshape turns out and moves down from mouth.

Can also mean—Heat

HOUR

Point right index finger up and rest knuckles on inside of open left hand; rotate the right hand around palm once.

HOUSE

Form inverted "V" with hands; draw hands apart and then down to imitate outline of roof and sides of house.

HOW

Touch backs of hands in front of chest, thumbs extended; curl hands out so that thumbs point forward.

HOW MANY?

Raise and open fists.

HUMBLE

Place side of right index finger at mouth, then lower hand and point fingertips at left palm from underneath.

Can also mean—Modest

HUNGRY

Slide "C" handshape down chest.

HUNTING

"L" handshapes move down twice.

HURRY

“H” handshapes move up and down twice.

Can also mean—Rush

HURT

Point index fingers together, with one palm facing down, the other facing up; rotate both hands so the positions are reversed.

Can also mean—Injure

HUSBAND

Touch thumb of open hand on forehead and move down to clasp left hand.

I

Point to center of chest with index finger.

Can also mean—Me

ICE CREAM

Move fist toward mouth as if holding an ice-cream cone, then down and back in a small circle. Repeat motion.

IDEA

Tip of little finger touches side of forehead and hand moves up and out.

Can also mean—Concept

IF

Make the "I" and "F" handshapes.

IGNORE

With palm in and fingers extended, touch nose with index finger and then move hand down and to the left.

Can also mean—Neglect

IMPATIENT

Hook index and middle fingers and rock hand back and forth across the back of left hand. Repeat motion.

Can also mean—Restless, anxious, edgy, agitated

IMPORTANT

Touch thumbs and index fingers of "F" handshapes together; raise hands, bringing hands out and back in together.

IMPOSSIBLE

"Y" handshape hits left palm. Repeat motion.

IMPROVE

Edge of right hand bounces twice up left forearm.

IN

Dip all five fingers into cupped hand.

INCLUDE

Stretch fingers to the side, then bring together and insert into cupped hand.

INCOMPETENT

Extend right fingers downward, grip thumb with left hand, and twist right hand up so that palm faces out.

INCREASE

Right "U" handshape rises and turns over to rest on left "U" handshape.

INDIVIDUAL

Place hands in front of chest, little fingers pointing out, and lower hands.

INFLUENCE

Closed handshape opens and moves forward from back of left hand.

INFORM

Close fingertips and touch right hand to forehead, left in front of face; bring hands out and away from body while opening fingers.

INNOCENT

Touch index and middle fingers of each hand to sides of chin at 45 degrees and move hands down and away from chin.

INSPIRED

Touch fingers to chest; raise hands and open fingers.

INSULT

Point index finger out, then up and forward.

Can also mean—Offend

INTERESTING

With palms in, right hand on top, thumbs and middle fingers near body, draw hands out while bringing thumbs and middle fingers together.

INTERRUPT

Push hand forward and down between thumb and index finger of edge of left hand.

INTERVIEW

Point little fingers up and alternately move hands toward and away from chin.

INTRODUCE

With palms facing up, point fingers across body, both arms wide apart; bring hands close together.

JAIL

Backs of spread right fingers tap forward twice against spread left fingers.

Can also mean—Prison

JEALOUS

Touch crooked index finger to side of mouth; turn finger around to point backward.

JUICE

Tip of little finger touches corner of mouth, then hand twists back and away.

JUMP

Stand right index and middle fingers on left palm; lift and bend fingers, then bring down again with fingers straightened.

KEEP

Right "K" handshape moves down onto left.

KEY

Rotate knuckle of right index finger forward against left palm. Repeat motion.

KICK

Using chopping motion, bring right hand up to strike left hand from below.

KILL

Point index finger down at 45 degrees and slide hand past left palm.

K

KIND

With palms in, rotate hands around each other in an outward circular motion starting near the heart.

**Can also mean—
Generous, gentle**

KISS

Closed fingertips touch together and then separate.

KITCHEN

"K" handshape turns over on left palm.

KNEEL

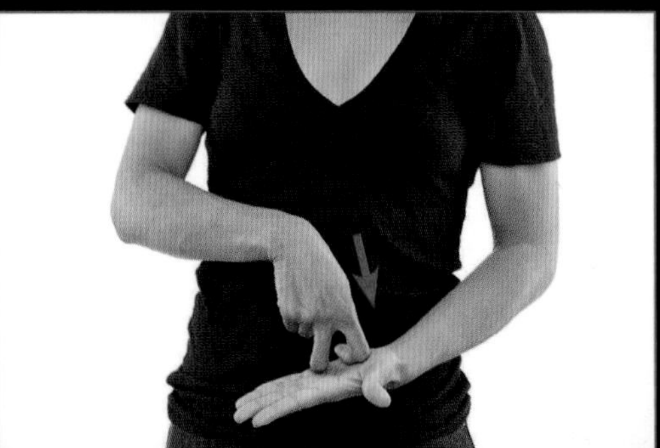

Stand knuckles of index and middle fingers on left palm.

KNIFE

Swipe middle finger of "U" handshape down and across index finger of left "U" handshape, as though sharpening a knife. Repeat motion.

KNOT

With thumbs against crooked index fingers, bring hands together. Right hand makes small circle and hands separate.

KNOW

Tap side of forehead twice with fingertips together.

LAMP

Place fingers together pointing down, then open fingers.

Can also mean—Light

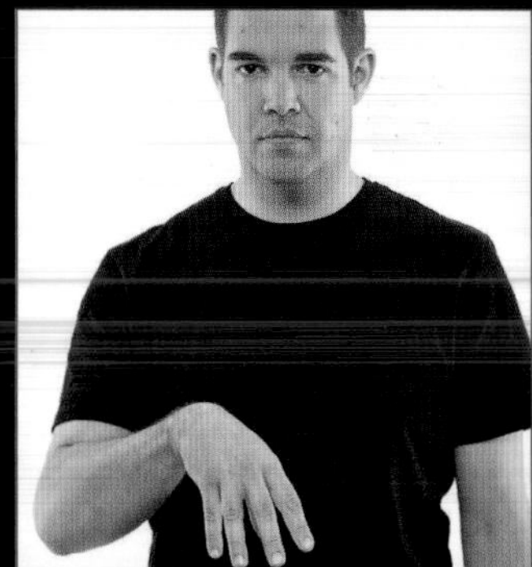

LANGUAGE

"L" handshapes meet at thumbs and separate as hands twist down and out slightly.

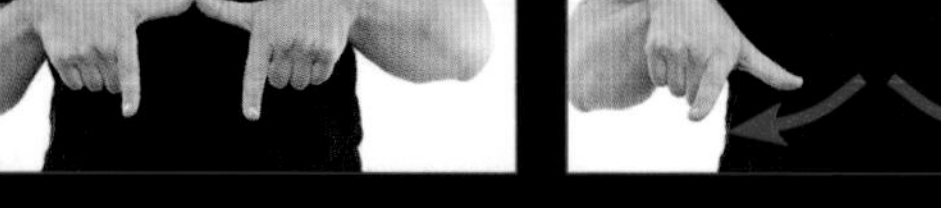

LAPTOP

Right palm sits on back of left hand, then moves up and turns to become vertical.

LAST (FINAL)

Right little finger touches left as it moves down at a right angle.

LATE (NOT ON TIME)

Palm points down and waves back twice.

LATER

Place thumb on left palm and point index finger up; twist thumb so index finger swivels forward and down.

LAUGH

Point both index fingers and brush outward and back from cheeks. Repeat motion.

LAW

Place right "L" handshape against left palm and bounce down once.

LAZY

Tap left shoulder twice with “L” handshape.

LEAD (GUIDE)

Clasp fingers of left hand and pull hands away from body.

LEARN

Spread fingers and rest on other palm; lift hand and bring fingers together on forehead.

LEAVE (BEHIND)

Move open hands forward and down.

LECTURE

Hold hand upright next to shoulder, then bring down and forward twice in a chopping motion.

LETTER

Point thumb to lips, then bring down on inside of left fingers, as though fixing a stamp to a letter.

Can also mean—Mail

LIBRARY

Move "L" handshape in two small clockwise circles in front of shoulder.

LICENSE

Thumbs of "L" handshapes tap together twice.

LIE

Move bent handshape from right to left under chin.

LIE DOWN

Fork middle and index fingers and draw back toward body across left palm.

LIGHT (WEIGHT)

Point middle fingers in; turn hands so that middle fingers point up.

LIGHTNING

Index finger moves downward in zigzag motion.

LIKE (PREFER)

Thumb and middle finger of open right hand touch chest, then join together as hand moves out.

LIKE (SIMILAR)

"Y" handshape, palm down, moves back and forth a few times.

LIMIT

With both bent handshapes pointing in, right over left, swivel hands at 90 degrees outward.

LIQUOR

With index and little fingers extended, underside of right hand comes down twice on top of left.

LIST (NOUN)

Tap inside of hand three times from left fingertips down left palm.

LISTEN

Place thumb of "C" handshape at ear.

LITTLE BIT

With knuckles facing out, rub tips of thumb and index finger together.

LIVE

Fists with thumbs extended slide up body.

LOCKED

Swivel right fist so that palm faces up, then lower onto back of left fist, wrist on wrist.

LONELY

Touch index finger to chin, then move down, forward and out in a circle. Repeat motion.

LONG

Draw index finger from left wrist to elbow.

LOOK AT

Fork index and middle fingers and move hand outward from face.

Can also mean—Watch

LOOK FOR

Rotate "C" handshape in two counterclockwise circles in front of face.

Can also mean—Search

LOSE (COMPETITION)

Lower "V" handshape onto left palm.

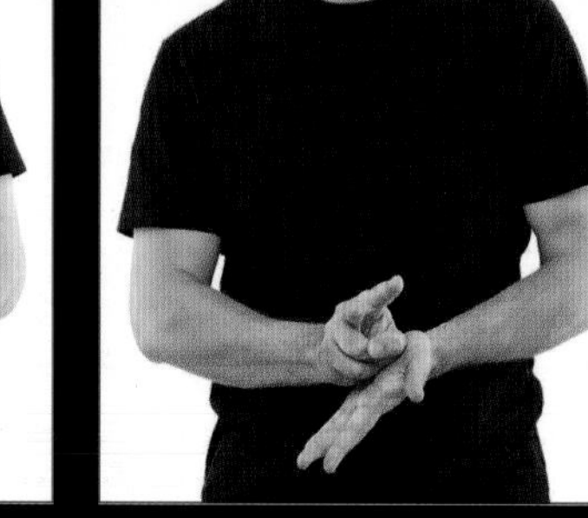

LOSE (MISPLACE)

Bent hands meet, backs of fingers touching, then open and pull apart.

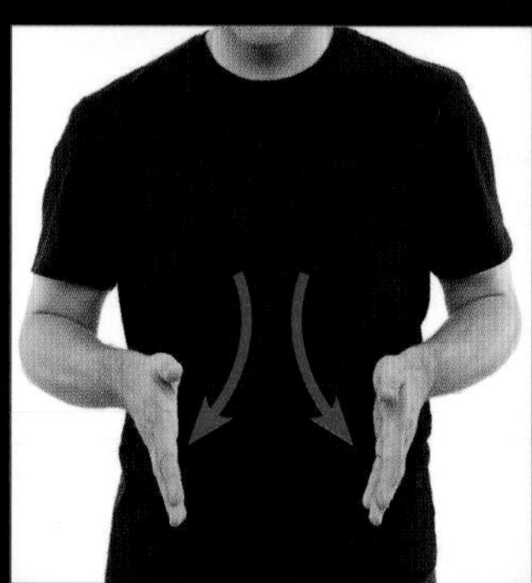

LOUSY

Touch thumb of "3" handshape to nose and bring hand right, left, and down.

Can also mean—Awful, terrible

LOVE

Cross fists at wrists and move toward body.

LOW

Flat hand moves down twice.

LUCKY

Middle finger touches chin and flicks down.

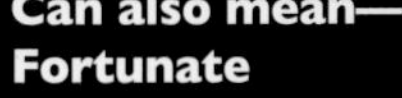
**Can also mean—
Fortunate**

LUNCH

Bring tips of fingers to mouth; straighten arm so that fingers point up and elbow rests on back of left hand.

MACHINE

Join hands together at knuckles to form "cog"; rock hands up and down.

Can also mean—Factory, motor

MAGAZINE

Slide thumb and knuckles of index finger up and down side of left hand twice.

MAKE (PRODUCE)

Place right fist on left, knuckles out; twist hands in, knuckles toward self.

MAN

Thumb of open hand touches forehead and moves down to chest.

MANY

“S” handshapes open as they move down.

MARRY

Start with hands apart, right higher than the left, and bring together in a clasp.

MATCH (FIRE)

Bring thumb and side of index finger together; place on palm of left hand and flick up, as if striking a match.

MATCH (FIT)

Bring knuckles together so hands interlock.

M

MATH

"M" handshapes move sideways so that they rub across each other twice.

MAXIMUM

Bring back of right hand up to meet palm of left hand.

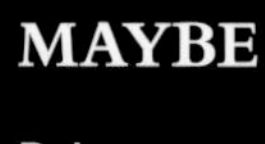

MAYBE

Palms up, alternately raise and lower hands at either side of body.

Can also mean—Probably

ME, TOO

"Y" handshape moves out from body twice.

MEAN (NASTY)

Touch nose with index finger, other fingers outstretched; bring hand down, curling in fingers to form fist, and strike past knuckles of left hand.

Can also mean—Cruel

MEANING

Fork index and middle fingers into palm; lift and twist fingers around so that back of hand faces out.

MEASURE

Bring tips of thumbs together and point out little fingers; tap thumbs together twice.

MECHANIC

Swivel index and middle fingers around left index finger.

Can also mean—Plumber

MEDICINE

Touch middle finger to left palm and rock hand from side to side.

MEET

Point index fingers up and bring hands together.

MEETING

Join hands by bringing thumbs together; fold fingers in so that tips touch twice.

Can also mean—Conference

MELT

Adjacent hands change from "O" to "A" handshapes as hands separate.

Can also mean—Dissolve, solve

MEMORIZE

Place fingertips on forehead and bring hand out to form fist.

MICROSCOPE

Tilt head down at an angle to look through cupped hands, right on top of the left; swivel hands back and forth as if adjusting magnification.

MICROWAVE OVEN

Point fists at each other, and then open and close fingers.

MIDDLE

Extended fingers rotate and lower to rest on left palm.

Can also mean—Center

MILITARY

With right hand higher than the left and thumbs extended, tap knuckles against side of chest twice.

MILK

Close fist twice.

MINIMUM

Right fingertips rise up from on top of left fingertips.

MINUTE

Right index finger clicks forward with hand against left palm.

MISS (FAIL TO CATCH)

Wide cup handshape sweeps down across face and closes to fist.

Can also mean—Guess

MISS (WISH TO SEE)

Touch index finger up to chin.

Can also mean—Disappointed

MISTAKE

Spread thumb and little finger; tap knuckles against chin twice.

Can also mean—Error

MOCK (RIDICULE)

Point index and little fingers out on both hands; jab hands forward twice.

MONEY

Tap back of closed handshape on palm twice.

MONTH

Back of right index finger slides down side of left index finger.

MOON

Form a half-round shape with thumb and index finger around eye; move hand up and out.

MORE

Tap fingertips of each hand together twice.

MORNING

Rest left hand inside right elbow; raise right arm from elbow.

MOST

With hands closed and thumbs extended, bring right hand up past left.

MOTHER

Tap chin twice with thumb of open hand.

MOTORCYCLE

Mime clutching handlebars; move knuckles of right hand backward and forward as though revving the engine.

MOUNTAIN

Rap back of left hand with knuckles; raise both hands at same angle with fingers outstretched.

MOUSE

Skim nose with index finger by moving hand across front of face twice.

MOVE (FROM/TO)

Closed handshapes move out in an arc.

MOVIE

With fingers stretched, palm facing out, and the heel of one hand resting on the fingers of the other, make a few back and forth waving motions.

MUSIC

Sweep fingers backward and forward over left arm.

MUST

Hook index finger and bring hand down.

Can also mean—Have to

MY

Press center of chest, palm facing in.

MYSELF

Thumb raised, press knuckles against center of chest twice.

NAME

Tap middle finger of right "H" handshape twice on index finger of left "H" handshape.

NEAR

Move back of right hand forward to palm of left hand.

Can also mean—Close (by)

NEGATIVE (ADJECTIVE)

Tap side of index finger twice against other palm.

NEPHEW

Place index and middle fingers next to side of head and swivel hand back and forth.

NERVOUS

Spread fingers and shake hands at either side of body.

NEVER

With palm starting at 45 degrees, swerve hand to right, then down.

NEW

With fingers bent in, strike knuckles across left palm.

NEWSPAPER

Bring back of thumb down on left palm while bringing index finger to thumb, and repeat.

Can also mean—Printing

NEXT (IN ORDER)

Lift right hand up and over left hand.

NEXT (TO)

Place right palm against left palm; move right hand to the right in a slight arc.

Can also mean—Neighbor

NICE

Wipe right palm across left palm.

NIECE

Place index and middle fingers next to chin and swivel hand back and forth.

NIGHT

Bend fingers at right-angle to palm; lower hand onto left wrist and bounce once.

Can also mean—Evening

NO

Thumb, index, and middle fingers close together.

NOISE

With both hands open, touch right index finger to ear and move both hands in and out twice.

NONE

"O" handshapes move out and down.

Can also mean—Nothing

NORTH

"N" handshape moves up.

NOSY

Touch index finger to nose and move down to hook into left "C" handshape.

NOT

Place thumb behind tip of chin and bring forward and slightly down.

Can also mean—Don't

NOTHING

Fist moves down and forward while opening.

NOTICE

Crook index finger and touch cheek below eye; bring finger down to left palm.

Can also mean—
Recognize

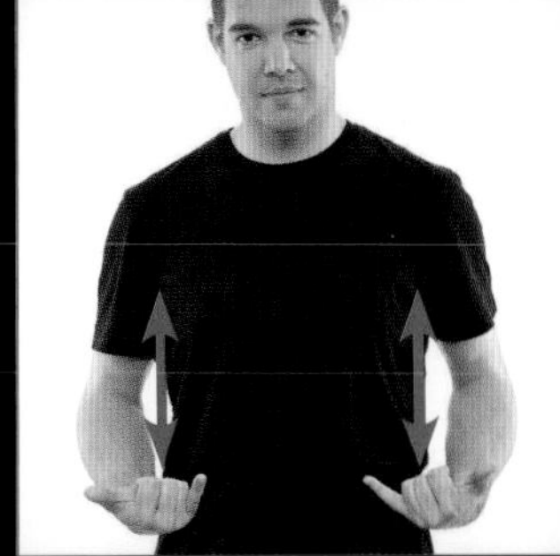

NOW

Stretch out thumbs and little fingers and lower hands twice.

NUMBER

Join hands by bringing fingertips together, one palm down, one up; swivel hands so that the palm positions are reversed.

NURSE

Tap index and middle fingers on left wrist twice.

OCCUR (TO)

Index finger touches side of forehead and swings down to rise up between index and middle fingers of left hand.

Can also mean—Realize

OF COURSE

Slap index and middle fingers down on back of left hand.

OFFER

Palms rise up and away from body.

Can also mean—Suggest

OFTEN

Bounce fingertips a few times out along palm of left hand.

Can also mean—Frequently

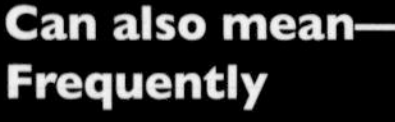

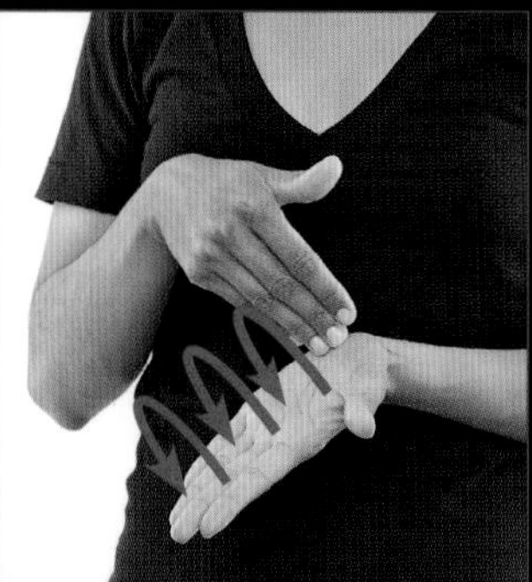
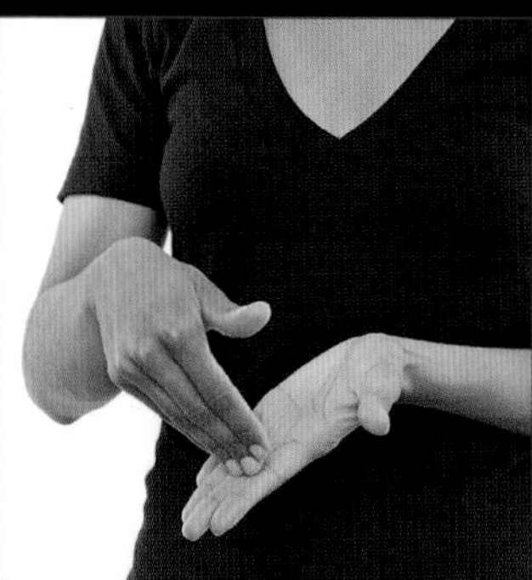

OLD

Place "C" handshape under chin; swerve hand down to chest and then straight down to waist while curling fingers to form fist.

ON

Right palm comes down on back of left hand.

ONCE

Flick index finger up from palm of left hand.

ONION

Touch knuckle of crooked index finger next to eye and swivel twice.

ONLY

Point index finger up, palm out; twist hand down and to the left and back up, finishing with palm in.

OPEN

Brings hands together, palms down; separate hands and turn palms over.

OPEN-MINDED

Cover forehead with fingers and swing both hands out.

Can also mean—Liberal

OPINION

With "O" handshape, pivoting from the wrist, slightly rock hand back and forth next to forehead.

OPPORTUNITY

Move hands forward, changing handshapes from "O" to "K."

OPPOSITE

Pull tips of index fingers apart.

OTHER

Point thumb to the left and rotate up over to the right.

Can also mean—Another

OUR

Cup hand with thumb against chest; arc hand across body so that little finger rests against left side of chest.

OUT

Lift closed hand out from cupped hand.

OVERHEAR

Place thumb to side of ear; curl index and middle fingers twice.

Can also mean—Eavesdrop

OVERLOOK

With palm in, wave hand down in front of face.

Can also mean—Miss (don't notice)

OVERWHELMED

Hands sweep up and over head.

OWE

Point index finger down at 45 degrees and tap left palm twice.

Can also mean—Afford, due, payable, unpaid, debt

PAINT

Sweep hand up and down from wrist twice as though it were a paintbrush.

PAPER

Strike right palm down and across left palm twice.

PARTY

"Y" handshapes swivel down and back twice.

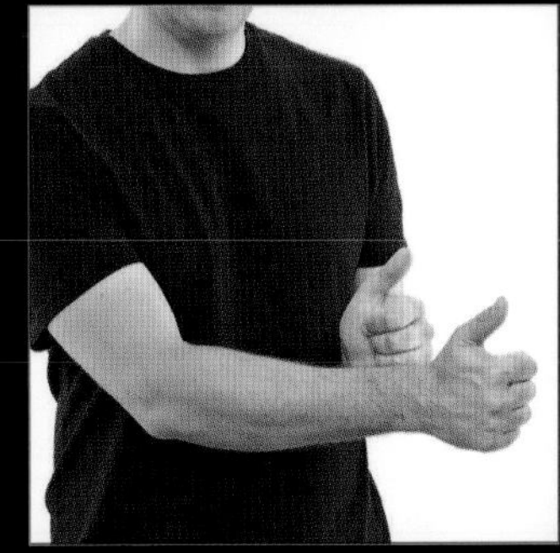

PASS

Thumbs up, knuckles out; move right hand ahead of the left.

PAST

Move hand back over shoulder and bend at wrist.

Can also mean—Previous, former

PASTA

Extended little fingers move up and in in two circles.

PATIENT (ADJECTIVE)

Thumb up, knuckles facing out; bring hand down from nose to chin twice.

Can also mean—Tolerant

PATIENT (NOUN)

Tip of middle finger of "P" handshape marks a cross on upper left arm.

PAY

Flick out index finger from left palm.

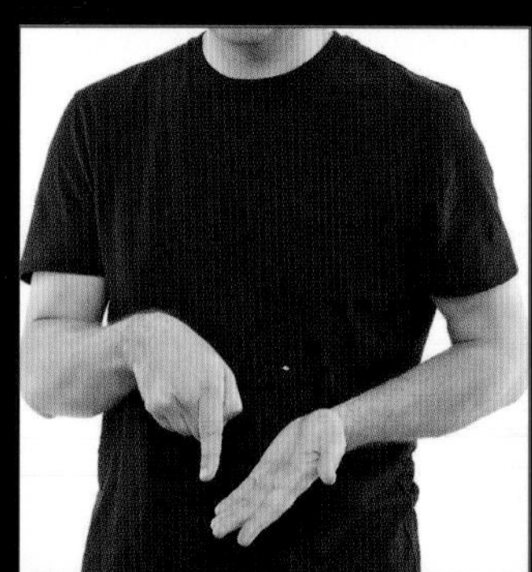

PAY ATTENTION

Place hands at side of head, palms facing in; move hands forward and down.

Can also mean— Concentrate

PEACE

Bring hands up so that insides of fingers meet, then reverse positions of hands before lowering and separating them.

PERFECT

Bring index finger and thumb together on both hands; circle right hand and bring tips of fingers down to left hand.

PERSON

Place hands at side of chest, palms facing in; move down body.

PERSONALITY

Make small circle with "P" handshape and bring to left shoulder.

PHOTOCOPY

Spread right fingers up so tips rest on left palm; bring right hand down while closing fingers together.

PHYSICS

Crooked middle and index fingers come together and touch twice.

PICTURE

Cup hand at side of face; bring down and place against left palm.

Can also mean—
Photograph

PIE

Slide edge of hand diagonally across left palm; repeat, sliding across at a different angle as though cutting a pie.

PITY

Point middle fingers down and rotate hands outward and back. Repeat motion.

Can also mean— Sympathy

PIZZA

Spread thumbs and index fingers as if holding a pizza; twist hands up and down twice.

PLACE (LOCATION)

Touch middle fingers of "P" handshapes in front of body; separate them, move them back, and then bring them together again.

PLAN

Point hands out at left side of body, right palm facing in; sway both hands down and up again to the right.

Can also mean—Organize

PLANT

Right hand opens as it moves up from inside left hand.

Can also mean—Spring (season)

PLATE

Both hands, with curved thumbs and index fingers, shake slightly.

PLAY (VERB)

With thumbs and little finger raised, rotate both hands out and back twice.

PLEASE

Hand rotates counterclockwise on chest.

POLICE

Cup hand and tap twice against left shoulder.

POLITE

Thumb gently strikes center of chest in the upward movement of each of two small up-and-out circles.

POLITICS

Middle finger of "P" handshape turns over and moves in to touch temple.

POPCORN

Alternately raise and lower hands, extending index fingers on the way up and retracting them on the way down.

POPULAR

Tap palm of cupped hand twice against side of vertically held index finger of left hand.

POSITIVE

Tap side of horizontal index finger twice against side of upright index finger of left hand.

POSSIBLE

Clench fists, knuckles out; move hands up and down twice.

POTATO

Crook index and middle fingers and tap twice on back of other hand.

POUR

"Y" handshape, thumb up, moves to left and turns over, so that thumb points down.

POWERFUL

Make wide cup shape with hand; tap against biceps of left arm and bring back out.

Can also mean—Strong

PRACTICE (REHEARSE)

With thumb extended, rub knuckles back and forth along index finger of other hand.

Can also mean—Train (practice)

PREDICT

Bring index and middle fingers close to face, then under and past left palm.

PREFER

Tap middle finger twice on chin.

PREGNANT

Spread fingers and place palm on abdomen; bring hand outward.

PRETEND

Place right palm on top of back of left hand; dip fingers forward.

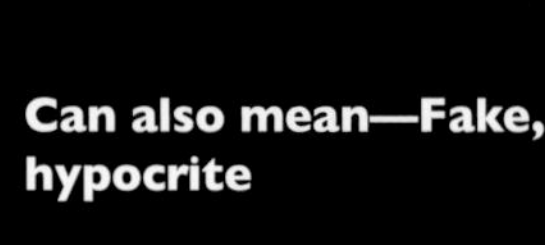

Can also mean—Fake, hypocrite

PRETTY

Open fingers at side of face; bring hand down past face while moving fingers together.

Can also mean—Beautiful

PREVENT

Cross right hand behind left and push out.

PROBLEM

Bring knuckles of index and middle fingers together and twist hands.

PROCEED

Place hands apart, palms in, and point fingers toward each other; move hands forward.

PROCESS

Rotate hands around each other in two forward circles.

PROFIT

Slide "F" handshape down torso, palm facing down.

Can also mean—Benefit

PROMISE

Bring side of index finger to lips; lower and open hand so that palm rests on left fist.

Can also mean—Guarantee

PROUD

Thumb slides up torso.

PROVE

Bring back of hand to opposite palm and bounce back up.

PUNISH

Strike a glancing blow against the left elbow with the right index finger.

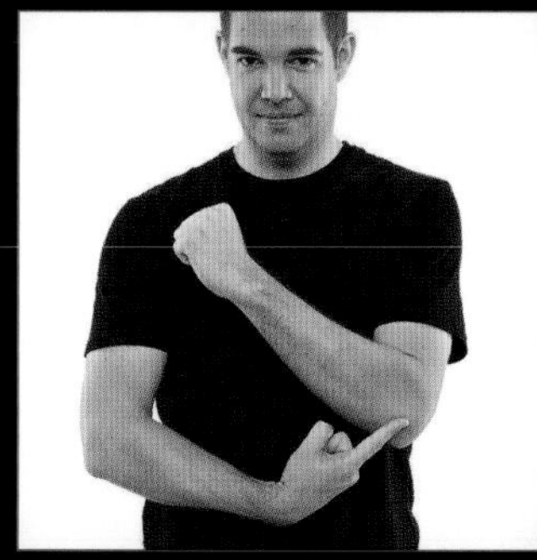

PURSE

Index finger arcs from left wrist to elbow.

Can also mean—Trash, garbage

PUT

Bring fingers of each hand together; lift and move both hands out and down again.

PUZZLED

Point index finger out, crook finger, and bring back against forehead.

QUARREL

Index fingers alternately move up and down at each other.

Can also mean—Argue

QUIET

Form an upside-down "V" shape with hands in front of mouth; bring hands out and down.

QUIT

Right index and middle fingers pull out of left fist.

Can also mean—Resign

RABBIT

Cross arms at wrists, palms in; fold in index and middle fingers twice.

RAIN

Move claw hands up and down twice from wrists.

READ

Point index and middle fingers at palm and sweep down twice from wrist.

READY

Move parallel "R" handshapes from left to right.

REAL

Place side of index finger on chin; bring hand forward and down.

Can also mean—Really, true, sure

REASON

"R" handshape describes two small circles next to forehead.

RECENTLY

Crook index finger twice on lower cheek.

Can also mean—Lately

REDUCE

Right index finger moves down near upturned left index finger.

Can also mean—Decrease

REFUSE

Raise thumb and bring straight back over shoulder.

REGULAR

Point index fingers diagonally out and tap hands together twice.

Can also mean—Typical, usual

REJECT

Point thumb up and then twist hand around to point down.

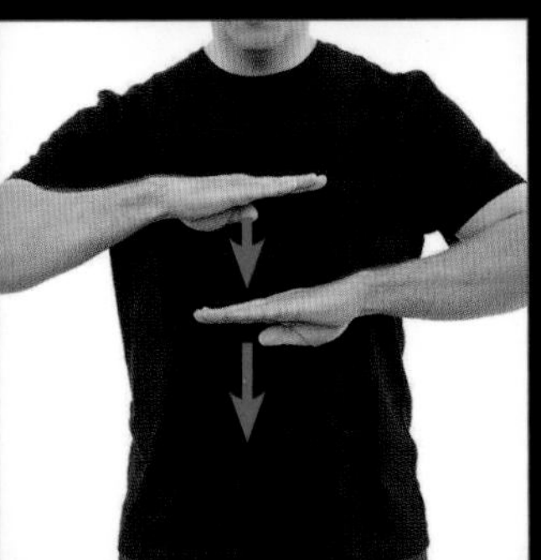

RELIEVED

Hands slide down torso.

RELIGION

Touch tip of "R" handshape to left shoulder; swing down and forward.

REMEMBER

Right thumb moves down from side of forehead to rest on back of other thumb and bounces once.

RESENT

Thumb of open hand flicks upward off of chest.

RESIGN

Move bent index and middle fingers up and out to the side of cupped left hand.

Can also mean—Quit

RESIST

Horizontal forearm and fist move away from body.

Can also mean—Defend, withstand

RESPONSIBILITY

Place fingertips of both hands on right shoulder and press down.

REST

Cross wrists in front of chest, palms facing in; tap hands twice against chest.

Can also mean—Relax

RESTAURANT

Touch fingertips of "R" handshape to one side of mouth and then the other.

R

RESTROOM

"T" handshape shakes sideways, back and forth.

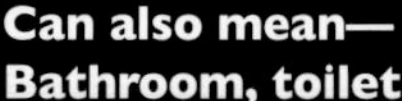

Can also mean— Bathroom, toilet

RETIRE (FROM WORK)

Stretch both hands in front of chest so that fingertips face each other; bring thumbs in to chest.

RICH

Raise back of closed hand up from left palm and open.

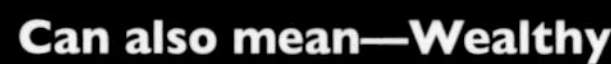

Can also mean—Wealthy

RIDE IN

Hook index and middle fingers over thumb of cupped left hand; use thumb to pull right hand forward.

RIDE ON

Fork middle and index fingers over edge of left hand; move hands forward.

RIGHT (CORRECT)

Point index fingers diagonally out; bring right hand down onto left hand.

Can also mean—Proper, appropriate

RIGHT (ENTITLEMENT)

Swivel edge of right hand up on left palm.

RIVER

Touch index finger of "W" handshape to chin; lower hand and then move both hands forward, right behind left, with fingers outstretched and wiggling.

ROAD

Parallel hands move forward.

ROOM

Place bent right hand in front of bent left; move hands around so that palms face each other.

Can also mean—Box

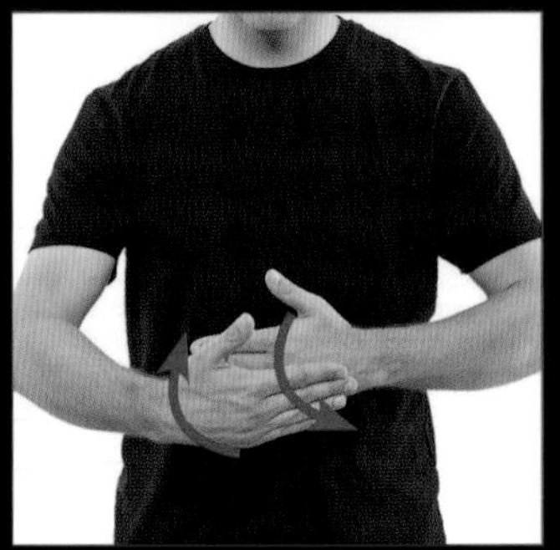

ROOMMATE

Fold fingers in and bring hands together so that knuckles interlock; repeat.

ROUGH

Brush fingertips of right claw handshape over left palm twice.

RUDE

Brush middle finger out over other palm.

RUIN

Crook index fingers; skim right hand out over left hand.

Can also mean—Spoil

RULE (POLICY)

Bounce fingertips of "R" handshape once down left palm.

RUN (EXERCISE)

Thumbs up, hook right index finger around thumb of left hand; push both hands out while crooking left index finger.

SAD

Open hands and lower from face.

SAFE (OUT OF DANGER)

Cross wrists, left over right, fists clenched in; uncross arms and rotate them out.

Can also mean—Save, rescue

SALAD

Two claw hands circle in, up, out, and around twice, as though tossing a salad.

SALT

Bring forked right hand down on left; wiggle right fingers alternately.

SAME

Bring index fingers to meet horizontally, side by side.

SANDWICH

Fold fingers of right hand over left, palms in; bring fingertips toward mouth twice.

Can also mean—Picnic

SATISFIED

Right hand above the left, palms down; bring hands to body.

Can also mean—Content

SAVE (KEEP)

Bring right "V" handshape up to back of left fist.

SAY

Tap index finger twice on chin.

SCHOOL

Bring right palm down onto left palm twice.

SCIENCE

Stick thumbs out so they face each other; alternately rotate hands in and around.

SCOLD

Wag index finger back and forward a few times.

SECOND (TIME)

Make "S," "E," and "C" handshapes.

SECRET

Tap lips twice with thumbnail.

Can also mean—Private, confidential

SECRETARY

Touch index and middle fingers to upper cheek; bring fingers down and slide out across other palm.

SEE

Touch middle finger of "V" handshape to cheek near eye; bring hand forward.

SEEM

Twist slightly curved hand backward and forward at side of head twice.

Can also mean—Apparently

SELFISH

Spread index and middle fingers and point out; bring hands in while hooking index and middle fingers under.

Can also mean—Greedy

SEMESTER

Fist near left shoulder moves to the right and down.

SEND

Brush fingertips out over back of left hand.

SENSITIVE

Touch middle finger to chest; flick finger slightly up and bring hand out and down.

SENTENCE

Bring index fingers and thumbs together so that both hands are joined; move right hand away.

SEPARATE

Touch backs of fingers together and pull them apart.

SERIOUS

Touch index finger to chin and twist.

SEVERAL

Arc hand out in front of body while opening fingers; keep thumb tucked in.

SHIRT

Grasp shirt near right shoulder with thumb and index finger; pull forward slightly twice.

SHOCKED

Touch forehead with index finger; lower hand so that both hands face down in slight claw shape.

SHOES

Clench fists and knock together twice.

SHOPPING

Closed right hand, thumb and fingertips touching, moves out from left palm a few times.

SHORT (HEIGHT)

Bent handshape bounces down twice.

SHORT (TIME)

Right index and middle fingers rest on those of the left hand and move back and forth twice.

Can also mean—Brief, soon

SHOULD

Hook index finger and move hand down twice.

Can also mean—Ought to

SHOUT

Claw fingers and bring to mouth; bring fingers up and away from mouth.

SHOWER

"S" handshape, up and to right of head, opens and moves down toward head twice.

SHY

Place back of fingers against cheek, fingertips pointing to chin; move hand forward while raising fingertips.

SICK

Touch right middle finger to forehead and left middle finger to stomach.

SIGN

Alternately rotate index fingers in toward self.

Can also mean—Sign language

SILLY

Stretch thumb and little finger; touch thumb to nose and flick hand down.

SIMILAR

"Y" handshape moves from side to side.

Can also mean—Too, also

SIMPLE

Bring thumb and index finger together on each hand; strike right fingers down past same fingers of left hand.

SINCE

Point index fingers back over right shoulder; bring hands forward and down.

SISTER

Extend index fingers and thumbs; lower right thumb from chin to rest right hand on left.

SIT

Hook index and middle fingers and lower onto same fingers of left hand.

SITUATION

Point index finger up; rotate right fist around finger.

SKILL

Clasp edge of left palm; pull clasping hand out to form "A" handshape.

SKIN

Pinch cheek with thumb and crooked index finger; shake slightly.

SLEEP

Bring open hand down past face and close fingers.

SLEEPY

Cup both hands, palms in; bring right hand down from eyebrows and near to left hand twice.

SLOW

Place right hand on back of left hand, palms down, and slide slowly up forearm.

SMALL

Bring palms close together twice.

Can also mean—Little

SMART

Touch forehead with index finger; raise finger up and forward.

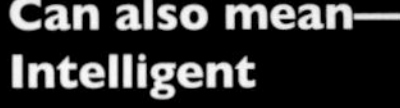

Can also mean—Intelligent

SMELL

Skim nose with inside of fingers twice using small forward circular motions.

SMILE

Touch fingers to either side of mouth; tilt hands up and smile.

Can also mean—Grin

SMOOTH

Rest fingertips of each hand on thumbs; move hands forward while sliding fingers into "A" handshapes.

SNOW

Spread fingers with palms out, hands at side of head; bring hands down while wiggling fingers.

SOAP

Brush fingertips across left palm twice.

SOCCER

Using chopping motion, raise hand to strike bottom edge of other hand twice at a right-angle.

SOCKS

Bring index fingers together, both pointing down; alternately slide fingers up and down past each other.

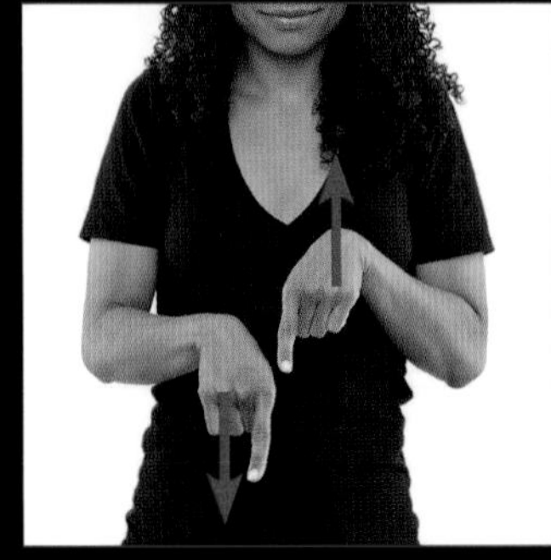

SODA

Dip middle finger into other clenched fist; remove middle finger and bring palm down.

SOFT

Lower open hands twice, closing hands on each downward movement.

SOMETHING

Raise index finger and rotate hand from elbow using small inward circular motions, keeping hand and finger vertical.

Can also mean—Someone

SOMETIMES

Flick index finger up from left palm twice.

Can also mean—Occasionally

SON

Side of right hand moves from forehead down to rest on left forearm.

SOON

Bring index finger and thumb together and tap chin twice.

SORRY

Rotate "A" handshape twice against chest.

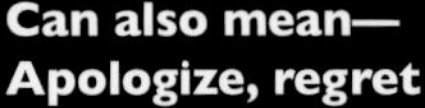
Can also mean— Apologize, regret

SOUTH

Bring fist down.

SPECIAL

Grab left index finger between right thumb and index finger and lift.

SPEECH-READ

Separated index and middle fingers move back and forth across mouth twice.

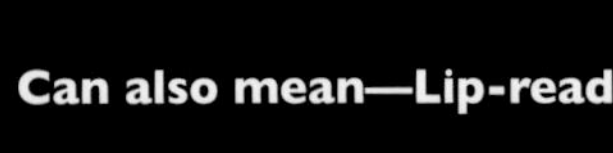
Can also mean—Lip-read

SPIDER

Cross right wrist down over left, fingers clawed; wiggle fingers while moving hands forward.

SPOILED

Right "X" handshape swings forward and up from left "X" handshape.

SPOON

Right "U" handshape moves up toward mouth twice.

STAIRS

Crook index and middle fingers; raise hand diagonally while making fingers "walk" up the stairs.

STAND

"Stand" index and middle fingers on left palm.

START

Twist index finger between index and middle fingers of left hand as hands move down.

Can also mean—Begin

STAY

Stretch thumbs and little fingers out so that thumbs meet in middle; bring right hand down.

Can also mean—Remain

STEAL

Touch left elbow with index and middle fingers of right hand; crook fingers and bring hand out and down.

STILL (CONTINUING)

Stretch thumbs and little fingers out; move hands down, forward, and up in an arc.

STOP

Bring edge of right hand down onto left palm.

Can also mean—Cease

STORE (SHOP)

Bring fingers together at either side of chest; swivel hands forward twice at wrists.

Can also mean—Market

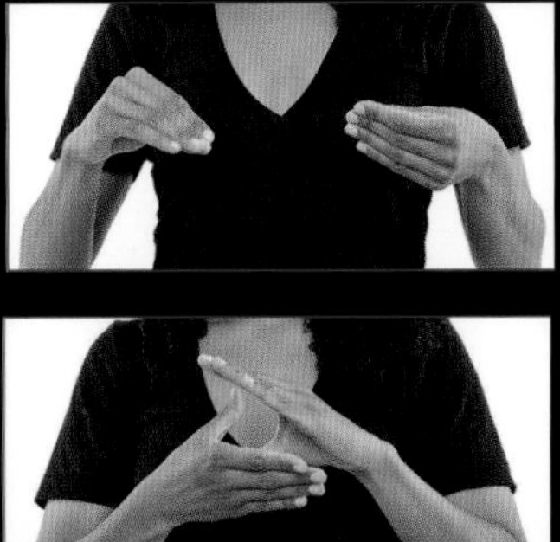

STORY (TALE)

Fingers together and thumbs apart; hands join at 90 degrees, then close and separate; repeat motion with hands in opposite positions

STRANGE

Cup hand, thumb beside cheek; sweep hand down in front of face.

Can also mean—Weird, peculiar

STRICT

Crook index and middle fingers; raise hand so that index finger rests on nose.

STUBBORN

Touch thumb on side of head, fingers upright; flap fingers forward and down.

STUCK

Bring index and middle fingers up to touch throat.

STUCK UP

Touch tip of index finger to nose and push head slightly back.

Can also mean—Snob

STUDENT

Place outstretched fingertips on left palm; lift hand, bringing fingers together, then drop and open fingers.

STUDY

Use fingertips to tap left palm twice.

STUPID

Bring back of index and middle fingers up to rest on forehead.

Can also mean—Ignorant

SUBTRACT

Close open hand into fist on left palm; move away, drop, and open.

Can also mean—Deduct

SUCCEED

Touch index fingers to either side of chin; bring hands out and sweep up to vertical.

Can also mean—Finally

SUFFER

Touch thumb to chin and twist twice.

SUGAR

Fingertips slide off of chin and down into palm.

SUMMARIZE

Open hands and stretch fingers, palms in; bring hands together as fists, right on top of left.

Can also mean—Condense

SUMMER

Lay index finger horizontally on forehead; pull finger across head while crooking finger.

SUN

Start with closed hand above and to right of head, palm out; twist palm in and open toward head.

SUNRISE

Fold arms in front of chest; raise cupped right hand up over left arm.

Can also mean—Dawn

SUNSET

Lower cupped right hand down past left arm.

Can also mean—Twilight

SUPERVISE

Make "V" handshapes, right resting on left; move hands together in two horizontal circles.

Can also mean—Manage, take care of

SUPPORT

Right fist pushes left fist up.

SUSPICIOUS

Index finger touches forehead above right eye, then moves out to crook. Repeat motion.

SWALLOW

Touch index finger to chin and slide finger down throat.

SWEEP

Fingertips of open hand brush back and forth across left palm.

SWEETHEART

Bring knuckles together, with thumbs extended; fold and unfold thumbs twice.

TABLE

Right arm bounces twice on left.

TAKE

Palm down, fingers outstretched; bring hand toward self while clenching fist.

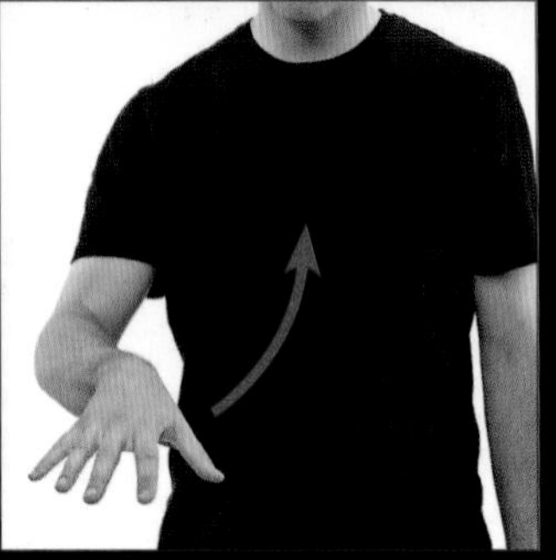

TAKE IT EASY

Hands outstretched, fingers pointing out; bob hands from side to side and up and down.

Can also mean—Relax

TALK

Index finger of "4" handshape taps chin twice.

Can also mean—Speak

TALL

Slide index finger up left palm.

TEA

Index finger and thumb together, dip twice in cupped left hand.

TEACH

"O" handshapes move forward and down twice from forehead.

TEAM

Thumbs of "T" handshapes meet in front of chest, then hands move out and back together while turning around.

TEETH

"X" handshape fingertip slides across teeth.

TELEPHONE

Bounce "Y" handshape twice on side of face.

TELEVISION

Make the "T" and "V" handshapes.

TELL

Touch tip of index finger to chin; bring hand forward and down.

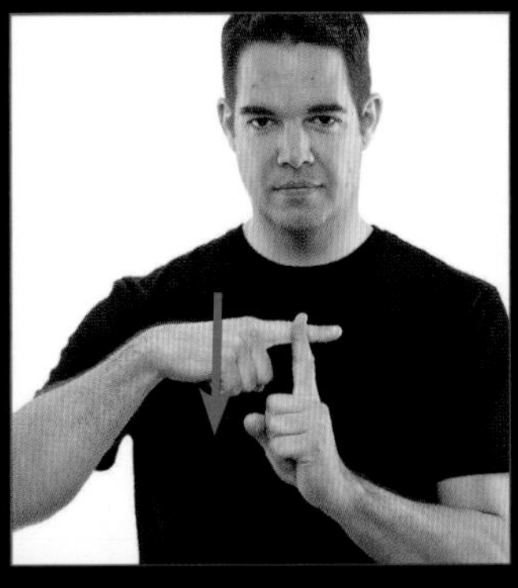

TEMPERATURE

Slide side of horizontal right index finger up and down side of vertical left index finger twice.

TEMPTED

Crook index finger and tap left elbow twice.

TEND (INCLINATION)

Middle finger touches chest, then moves out and down to the left.

TERRIBLE

Bring index finger and thumb together on both hands; flick fingers open.

Can also mean—Horrible

TEST

Point index fingers up at shoulder level; lower hands while crooking fingers, then spread fingers down.

Can also mean—Exam

TEXT (MESSAGING)

"A" handshape thumbs alternate up and down.

THAN

Swipe right hand down so that fingertips slap left fingertips.

THANK YOU

Hand moves forward and down from chin.

THANKSGIVING

Point index finger and thumb down from chin and move hand down to chest.

THAT

Move "Y" handshape down.

THEIR

Palm sweeps around in an arc.

THEY

Index finger sweeps around in an arc.

Can also mean—Those, these

THICK

Make hand a wide claw shape and bring fingertips to cheek.

THIN

Thumb and index finger move down.

Can also mean—Slim

THING

Slightly cup hand, palm up; bounce twice to the right.

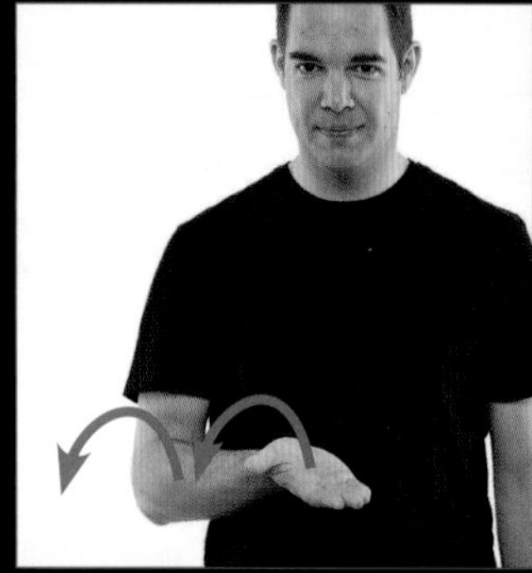

THINK

Touch index finger to side of head.

THIRSTY

Slide index finger along throat, top to bottom.

THRILLED

Touch middle fingers to either side of chest; briskly flick hands apart and up.

Can also mean—Excited

THROUGH

Slide edge of hand through and between index and middle fingers of left hand.

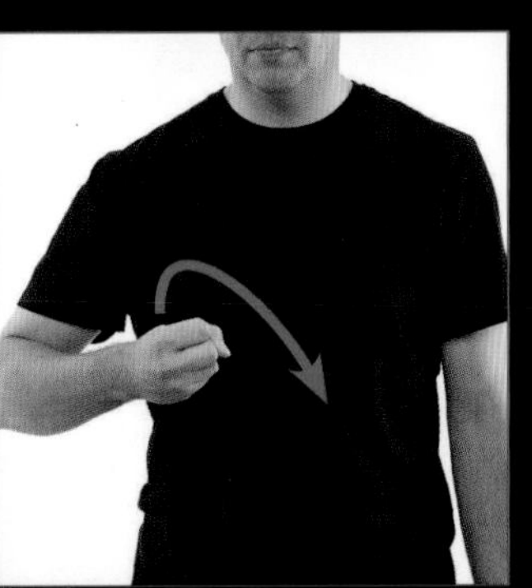

THROW AWAY

Flick index and middle fingers out straight from the fist.

Can also mean—Discard

THUNDER

Touch ear with index finger, then alternately rock fists in and out at chest level.

Can also mean—Loud

TICKET

Crooked index and middle fingers of right hand punch edge of left hand twice.

TIME

Crooked index finger moves down to back of other wrist.

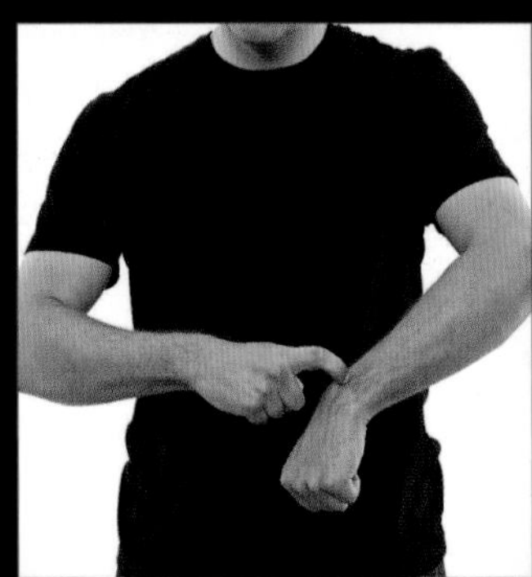

TIRED

Touch bent fingers to either side of chest, thumbs up; twist hands down from fingertips.

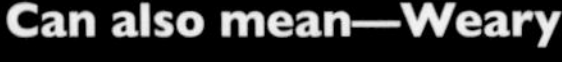
Can also mean—Weary

TODAY

"Y" handshapes move down, and then right arm with index finger extended moves down onto left arm.

TOGETHER

"A" handshapes meet and move up and down together slightly.

TOMORROW

Thumb touches right side of cheek and swings forward.

TOUCH

Middle finger taps back of left hand.

TRAIN (LOCOMOTIVE)

Slide index and middle fingers up and down back of same fingers on left hand twice.

TRASH

Tap palm twice against side of head.

Can also mean—Lettuce

TRAVEL

Crook index and middle fingers; rotate hand in small counterclockwise horizontal circles while moving up and to the left.

Can also mean—Trip

TREE

With right elbow resting on back of left hand, spread fingers and waggle right hand.

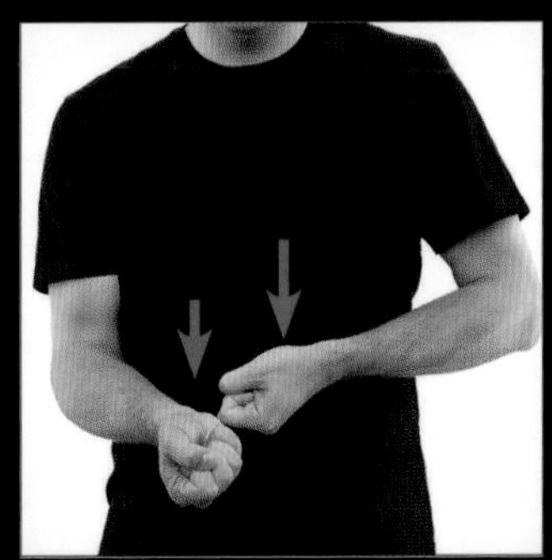

TRUST

Stretch fingers, left hand above the right, palms in; curl fingers to form fists and move hands down.

TRY

"A" handshapes at chest swivel down and forward.

Can also mean—Attempt

UGLY

Place crossed index fingers in front of chin; move hands apart while crooking fingers.

UMBRELLA

Place right fist on top of left; raise right hand and bring back down to left hand.

UNCLE

"U" handshape moves in two small circles at side of head.

UNDER

Right "A" handshape moves down under left palm.

Can also mean—Below

UNDERSTAND

Snap index finger up from fist next to head.

UNTIL

Bring tip of right index finger down to touch tip of left index finger.

Can also mean—To

UPSET

Place palm on stomach and flip over.

USE

Make two circles with "U" handshape on back of left fist.

Can also mean—Wear

VACATION

Fingers stretched, touch thumbs to either side of chest twice.

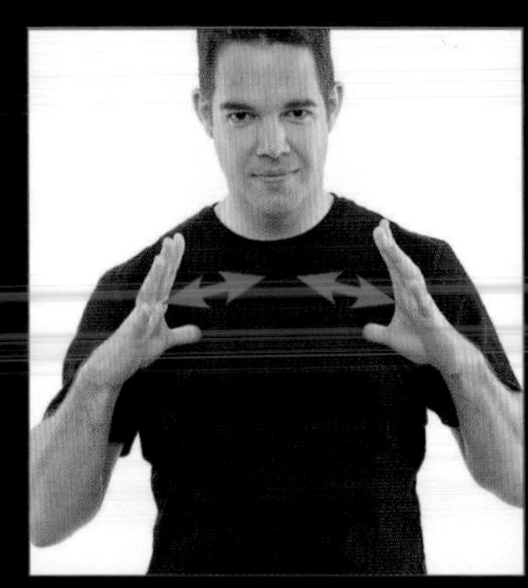

VAGUE

Fingers stretched, rub palms together using a circular motion.

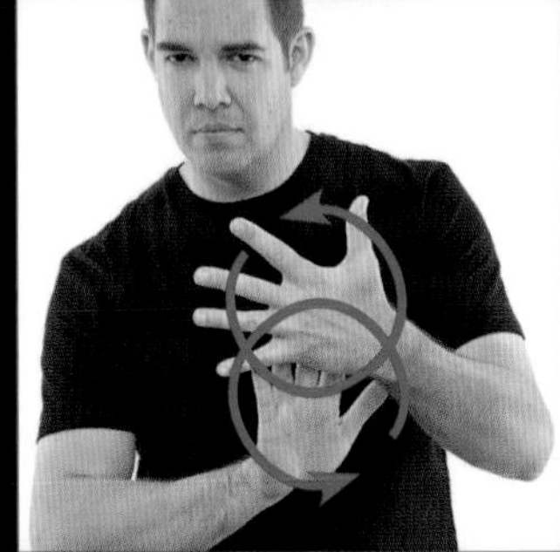

VERY

"V" handshapes meet at fingertips and separate.

VISIT

"V" handshapes rotate alternately using an outward circular motion.

WAIT

Raise both hands to left side, palms facing up; move hands in small forward circles while wiggling fingers.

WALK

Hands alternately rock back and forth to mimic motion of feet.

WANT

Move claw hands in toward body while crooking all ten fingers.

WARM

Move fingertips of closed hand out from mouth while opening fingers.

WARN

Tap back of hand twice.

WASH

Bring knuckles together; scrub top hand back and forth over left hand a few times.

WATER

Tap chin twice with index finger of "W" handshape.

WE

Touch index finger to right side of chest and then arc over to left side.

Can also mean—Us

WEAK

Touch tips of spread fingers to left palm; bend and unbend fingertips into palm twice.

WEB SITE

Extended middle fingertips touch and then hands rock alternately back and forth.

Can also mean—Internet

WEEK

Side of right hand, with index finger extended, slides along left palm.

WEIGH

Place index and middle fingers across same fingers of left hand; tilt top fingers backward and forward twice.

WEST

"W" handshape moves across body to the left.

WET

Bring both hands in front of chest, palms in, fingers up, and close fingers twice.

WHAT?

Open hands and stretch fingers, palms up; move hands back and forth.

WHEN?

Right index finger circles clockwise down onto left index finger.

WHERE?

Wag index finger two or three times.

WHICH?

Thumbs up, back of hands facing out; alternately move hands up and down.

WHO?

Touch thumb tip of "L" handshape on chin; crook index finger twice.

WHY?

Touch hand to side of head; bring hand down to "Y" handshape.

WIFE

Touch thumb tip of cupped right hand to right side of chin; bring hand down to clasp left hand.

WILL

Move hand forward from side of head.

WILLING

Place hand on chest; move out and down so palm faces up.

WIN

Right claw hand mimes grabbing something from left fist and moves up.

WIND

Hands move from side to side with fingers spread.

WINDOW

Palms in, bring edge of right hand down onto left hand and repeat.

WINE

Rotate "W" handshape in small forward circles at cheek.

WINTER

Fists move in small outward circles.

WISH

Cupped hand slides down chest.

WITH

"A" handshapes move together once.

WITHOUT

Make the sign WITH, then separate hands while spreading fingers.

WOMAN

Thumb of open hand moves from chin down to chest.

WONDERFUL

Palms out, move hands forward, back, and forward again.

Can also mean—Great, fantastic

WOOD

Use edge of hand to mime sawing on back of other hand.

WORD

Tap extended thumb and index finger twice on left index finger.

WORK

Tap right wrist twice down onto back of left wrist.

Can also mean—Job

WORLD

Right "W" handshape circles outward around left "W" and comes to rest on it.

WORRY

Alternately rotate "B" handshapes in toward face.

WORSE

"V" handshapes cross each other, left in front of right.

Can also mean—Multiply

WRITE

Bend thumb and index finger together; drag across left palm.

WRONG

Bring knuckles of "Y" handshape up to touch chin.

YEAR

Right fist circles forward around left fist and comes to rest on top.

YES

Bend fist down twice.

YESTERDAY

Extended thumb touches jaw near chin and moves back.

YOU

Point index finger out.

YOUNG

Fingers touch chest near shoulders and flick up twice.

YOUR

Palm out, push hand forward.

Lauren Ridloff is a native Chicagoan. She attended Model Secondary School for the Deaf in Washington, D.C., and continued her education at California State University, Northridge, graduating with a bachelor's degree in English. In 2000 Lauren was crowned as Miss Deaf America. Upon completion of her reign, she received her master's in education at Hunter College in New York City. Lauren resides in Brooklyn and taught at a public school in Manhattan. However in 2017 she swapped the classroom for the stage appearing as Sarah Norman on Berkshire Theatre Group's production of *Children of a Lesser God*, a role which she reprised in 2018 on Broadway opposite Joshua Jackson.

Darren Fudenske was born in Brooklyn, New York. He received his bachelor's degree in English from Gallaudet University in Washington, D.C., and his master's in deaf education from Hunter College in New York City. He currently teaches at a public school and lives in Manhattan. Darren has appeared in off-Broadway shows, films, and television, including *Law & Order: Criminal Intent* and *Rescue Me*.